CW01203262

ISBN 978-0-331-00809-8
PIBN 11001605

NOTES AND QUOTES

For Administrative Use Only February 1949

RECOGNITION MEETINGS SHOW VALUE OF SUPERVISION

Final returns are in from many of the major "Recognition Meetings", and again Farmers Home Administration families showing the benefits of supervised credit, competed successfully with other farmers.

- - - - - - - - - - - - - - - - - - - -

OTHERS CAN HELP YOU

Arkansas State Director Highfill is a firm believer in the theory that his supervisors can make their own jobs easier if they get others to help them. Take for example the problem of obtaining rent free space for county offices. In Arkansas the County Quorum Courts and the Justices of the Peace have a good deal to say about the allocation of space in local government buildings. Recently Highfill noted that the County Quorum Courts would be meeting throughout Arkansas early in January, and urged all of his supervisors to appear before the courts and tell them about the contribution the Farmers Home Administration makes to the local community. He reasoned that if the Courts thoroughly understood the value of Farmers Home they would be more willing than ever to make office space available to the agency.

Highfill suggested to his county supervisors that they take the Chairman of their local county committee with them when they appeared before the Court. He pointed out that in some instances they might assign the committeeman the job of making the report on the agency's activities to the Court.

(CONTINUED ON PAGE SIX)

During 15 years of Plant-To-Prosper competition, for example, Farmers Home borrowers have won many of the major prizes in a contest where this year over 46,000 Mississippi-valley farmers competed.

In the companion Live-At-Home contest held for Negro families other present or former borrowers are showing that the training and opportunity they received through this agency is paying off cash-award dividends as well as improved standards of living.

In Arkansas' more recently established Balanced Farming Competition, the show was almost an FHA-family affair with four of the six top awards going to borrowers or families who had received their earlier training with us.

Almost every year an Ohio FHA family is selected as one of the top winners in the Cleveland Farmers competition for "best in the state". And FHA families are frequently included in "Outstanding Farmer" selections made by several southern farm magazines. We weren't surprised, recently, when State Director Newton of Maryland-Delaware told us that the son of a tenant purchase borrower was chosen international livestock judging champion.

(CONTINUED ON PAGE TWO)

There is a lot of satisfaction in knowing that our program is capable of developing families to the point where they can be selected as the best farmers of their classification in a state or in a several-state area. And there's an ever greater satisfaction in knowing that the principles of better-farming-for-better-living upon which we have based our supervision is being recognized widely as the pattern upon which selection of outstanding families should be made. Most valuable of all is the inspiration provided other borrowers to make an equally worthwhile record.

Some folks say "We can't really claim credit for the accomplishments of these families". They go on to say such things as "Other agencies made major contributions, too" or "They are exceptional families, they would have won anyway". And whenever we hear such statements we remember the time we interviewed an FHA-borrower family from Missouri who had just won the Plant-To-Prosper Sweepstakes.

Winning Family Gives FHA Credit

This family told us "We are proud we won the prize, but we're mighty humble, too, when we think back over the past. Do you really think we could have won it if we had stayed where we were when you folks gave us our first boost? Maybe what we did was important, but what you did in giving us the opportunity should be recognized. We can't even take too much credit for what we did, because you helped us there, too. We didn't have a chance to go to school and learn how to farm right, but you brought the school right to us. You helped us plan how to operate this old farm; got us a long-time lease on it so we could actually do some of the things you said should be done. You showed us how to plant cover crops, stretch our feeding season by growing supplemental pasture crops, and convert from a cotton-farm to a cotton and dairy farm. You set up books so we could kee records of what we were doing, and helped us figure out what those records meant'

It Doesn't Rob Others Of Deserving Credit

The family meant that tribute to our supervised credit. They weren't taking credit away from themselves or from any of the others who had also helped them. For example, they told us that the "County Agent helped us a lot, too. We didn' know about him, or what he could do for us until you folks brought him out to o farm. Since then we've gone to a lot of the meetings he's held, and learned a lot that helped us. But we'd never have gone that first time, probably, if you hadn't suggested that we do."

Maybe you, the supervisor, can't take ALL the credit when a family is selected a outstanding farmer in their state or group of states. But for any farmer to get that high on the agricultural ladder, he needed a lot of help. He knows it, an so do you. If he thought it would help other farmers do as well, he'd tell the about it. Then why shouldn't you, who DO know many farmers who could use those same services, point with pride to what some outstanding farmer was able to accomplish with your aid. If it helps the other farmers who need your aid, the telling them about it is part of your job, too.

Here are some of the things which we did help farmers do, and the recognition they won for their accomplishments.

FHA Borrowers Are Among Top Winners

The Memphis Commercial Appeal's twin contests--Plant-to-Prosper and Live-at-Home --are the daddy of all contests, and should be mentioned first.

Second and third place in the Tennessee competition were won by the James J. Sims family of Brownsville, who purchased their 90 acre family-type farm through the FHA, and the Paul Auston family of Dyer, who had purchased a 50 acre farm with our aid. Two FHA borrowers and a County FHA committeeman were among the group in Tennessee who received honorable mention.

A Tennessee Negro FHA family--William Ragland of Denmark--won first in the state in Live-at-Home, followed closely by two other FHA borrowers who placed second and third.

The same story could be told of each of the four states in which the Plant-to-Prosper and the Live-at-Home operates. Missouri, placed FHA borrowers first and second in the Live-at-Home Negro competition, and first and fourth in the Plant-to-Prosper landowner division. In Arkansas, top winner in both landowner and tenant divisions went to present or past borrowers.

FHA Personnel Honored For Part In Winning

FHA personnel also came in for honors at the Sweepstakes finals held in Memphis last month. Itawamba County, Mississippi, was recognized for its efforts in securing the largest number of entries of any county, and supervisor Roy F. Robinson of that county was presented with a trophy. Supervisor Bob Scruggs, of Henry County, Tennessee, was one of the trophy recipients for his part in the county work which developed the sweepstake winner.

On the speaker's platform for one of the principal talks was Marcus Braswell, Production Loan division chief from Washington. Each year recently Farmers Home has been recognized, and as per usual the reports coming back from Memphis were that Braswell's talk was the best of a mighty fine lot of speeches.

Also present at the speaker's table were State Directors Beasley of Tennessee, Carpenter of Missouri, Fatherree of Mississippi, and Highfill of Arkansas as well as several members of their staff.

Arkansas Balanced Farming Competition Has FHA Winners, Too

Arkansas State Director J. V. Highfill, reports that FHA borrowers won most of the prizes in the Balanced Farming contest for 1948. This competition, the second annual held in the state, is aimed at better production on the farm, making farm buildings more healthful and habitable and developing a "live at home" program so that families can grow on their farm the foods they eat or preserve for off-season consumption.

Newspapers in the State of Arkansas, long one of the competing states in the "Plant-to-Prosper" program sponsored by the Memphis Commercial Appeal, two years ago instituted a similar program of their own, not to compete with the original "Plant-to-Prosper" contest but to give further recognition to the thousands of farm families of Arkansas, who had yearly taken part in the much larger competition. Under the sponsorship of the Arkansas Press Association and with the cooperation of Arkansas Power and Light Company, the Agricultural Extension Service, the Farmers Home Administration and the Memphis Commercial Appeal, the Second Annual Balanced Farming Contest was held in Little Rock on December 8, 1948. Contests are on a county basis, with all county winners competing for state champions. In contests such as the "Plant-to-Prosper", sweepstake champions are later selected on an area-wide basis from among the state first, second and third place winners.

This contest is open to all farm families in the State, both Negro and white, including the 15,000 farm families who are using the facilities of the Farmers Home Administration. Mr. Highfill, in expressing his pleasure for the participation of the FHA in the Balanced Farming contest, as well as having a part in the meeting at which time the awards were made, called attention to the fact that such competition helps farmers enjoy many of what he describes as "the better things of Life", the goal the FHA in Arkansas agriculture has been striving for for many years.

As in last years competition, in this years' contest Farmers Home borrowers or former borrowers, won a majority of the awards. In the Landowner Division where three top prizes were given, Farmers Home families took first and third places; in the Tenant Division first, second, and third places were won by either borrowers or former borrowers. In the Plantation Division, another Division in the competition, we had no borrowers.

Highfill Keynotes Award Presentations

In his address to the membership of the Contest Committee, the winners and the guests who had assembled for the awards, Mr. Highfill, who is a strong proponent for any farm program that makes for a better home and better living, said: "I want to congratulate the winners in this contest as well as all families who entered the contest throughout the State, for it is my feeling that all entrants, whether they were winners or not, gained by their participation in this worthwhile undertaking........the plans which the agricultural leaders of the State have had for many years, as well as the objectives that farm people have had for many years, are now beginning to pay dividends. They are dividends that to me, and I am sure to you, mean better living.

"I would like to repeat again those things that will be achieved through balanced farming--Conservation of human resources; Proper land use, as well as the conservation of our soil and its resources; It will strengthen the entire agricultural economy of Arkansas; Balanced farming will bring about greater parity of opportunity for farm people; It will correct many of the maladjustments or disparities which exist on farms to-day; and it will bring about greater opportunity for physical, mental and spiritual developments as well as happiness and contentment on the farms through Arkansas."

FHA families among the winners included:

Mr. and Mrs. James R. Black - of Arkansas county who won the Landowner Division. A year ago the Blacks bought a 145-acre farm near Humphrey, Arkansas County, through a Farmers Home Administration loan, and will complete payments this year. The farm had no house. They bought one at Lake Dick, moved it to the farm, and remodeled it.

Despite a blight Mr. Black produced 51 bushels of rice per acre last summer compared with the state's average of 48. His other major crops were oats and soybeans. Mrs. Black has a 650-pound capacity home freezer containing 45 chickens, two hogs and a beef. A permanent pasture has been started in preparation for a beef herd.

An award of $200 will be presented Mr. and Mrs. Black by the Arkansas Power and Light Company and the Memphis Commercial Appeal, which with the state Extension Service and Farmers Home Administration, are aiding the Arkansas Press Association in sponsoring the competition.

Eugenia McJunkins - of Route 4, Marianna, a 42-year old, single Negro woman, who has been sole operator of a farm for 15 years, was named winner in the Home Improvement division at the second annual luncheon and forum of the Live-at-Home division of the Arkansas Balanced Farming competition.

The announcement, made at the meeting held in the Arkansas Baptist College, said she got her start on the 14 acres of farmland when a tenant family moved and left a crop in the fields. Eugenia picked six bales of cotton on the land that year.

Although her home burned four years ago, she now has built a nice five-room house in its place. The house is furnished with comfortable, sturdy furniture.

Eugenia's first-place award today was for the improvements she made to her home during the past year. These improvements included the painting of a portion of the interior, wiring the house for electricity and purchasing of two large fans and a radio. She was awarded a $50 prize.

"I plan to stay in the live-at-home contest," she said, "I've just begun to farm."

By planting vetch during the winter on the six acres of the farm devoted to cotton, Eugenia has increased the yield to one and one fourth bales an acre. With the money earned from the land, Eugenia has bought five lots and rents houses in Marianna. She owns a tractor and a jeep.

Mr. and Mrs. W. R. Valentine - of Route 6, Paragould, Greene County, in winning first place in the Tenant-Sharecropper Division, exhibited the benefits to be derived from diversification in farming. The family, including Billy Gene, 15, and Dale, nine, worked together to improve their home during the past year.

They installed an electric lighting system, painted and redecorated the interior of their home and leveled the yard and planted shrubbery.

The Valentines moved to their 80-acre farm in 1941 and built their house the same year. Realizing the importance of a balanced farm program, Mr. Valentine got permission from the farm owner to diversify his operation instead of raising cotton only.

Now, only about 25 per cent of the land is devoted to cotton, with the rest used for a combination crop of corn and soybeans, which provide most of the feed for hogs, the family's other big source of income. At present they own 44 hogs.

"We now realize that tenants can live on a farm as well as anyone," Mr. Valentine said, "so long as it is well planned and organized to its best advantages." He keeps a record book, uses a sound crop rotation system and builds up his land by planting pasture crops and using vetch as a winter cover crop.

Son Of Borrower Wins Arkansas Livestock Show Championship

Ten calves purchased last year with a Farmers Home Administration loan by Floyd Wren of Prescott have paid prize-winning dividends this year. Mr. Wren's 17-year old son, Joe, developed the winning calves in his work as a member of the Future Farmers of America. "Victory Tone", Joe's 1,125 pound Hereford steer, was Southwest Arkansas Champion at Hope and Grand Champion at the Four-State Fair at Texarkana and finally was crowned Grand Champion of the Junior Division of the 1948 Arkansas Livestock Show at Little Rock. The champion steer sold for the all-time record price of $1.51 a pound at the annual auction. With this and other entries of steers and heifers, Joe Wren won 2 first, 2 second, and 2 third places in the Arkansas Livestock Show, which earned for him about $2,900 in cash and a registered Hereford heifer. This is Joe's third year in FFA work.

New Jersey Farmers Week Recognizes Borrower Accomplishments

Again Farmers Home Administration officials and borrowers had a prominent place in New Jersey's 1949 Farmers Week. On Wednesday, January 26, Administrator Lasseter was the principal speaker at a luncheon conference. Dr. W. H. Martin, director of the New Jersey Experiment Stations, awarded citations to FHA borrowers who made outstanding progress during the previous year. State Director Tyson has been making a series of color slides which show the work being done on borrower farms in various parts of the state, and we understand that he showed these slides as part of the week-long program dedicated to New Jersey agriculture

******

OTHERS CAN HELP YOU (Continued from page 1)

The report should be brief, not more than 15 minutes in length. It should contain all the pertinent facts about the agencies activities including, number and amount of loans made, increase in net worth and purchasing power of borrowers, amount of funds collected, and examples of progress made by borrowers, especiall in ability to pay taxes, take part in community affairs, and otherwise assume the duties of citizenship.

******

Notes and Quotes Index for 1948

Several of you have asked for an index which told quickly where to find the material in past issues of Notes and Quotes that might be helpful to you in your state or county operations. The following index will, we believe, tell you where you can find items of interest on several subjects:

******

"They Renew Your Faith in Farming"

The Southern Planter for October, 1948 carried an article by P. M. Jackson, about a North Carolina couple, who purchased a 54-acre farm with a loan from the Farmers Home Administration.

When Mr. and Mrs. Wade Alexander moved to their new 54-acre farm near Asheville, North Carolina, in January of 1944 they had only a net worth of $3,300 but did have an experience of over 14 years of tenant farming back of them. Their Farmers Home loan brought with it a hard, backbreaking job. Land grown up to brush, soil eroded and leached, no decent pasture, a damaged dwelling, no suitable fencing!

With the help of Kelly Ray, Buncombe County supervisor for the Farmers Home, and other agricultural agency people, the Alexanders started in earnest. Improvement of the soil was imperative, and, with lime, lespedeza and hard labor they began a four-year rotation of corn, wheat and grass. They built a poultry house and corn crib increasing their flock of fowl to over 400 and they harvest some 70 bushels of corn to the acre. They now sell cattle, eggs and poultry, hogs and tobacco. Their dairy products alone bring in a good income; their land has doubled and trebled in its yield.

In December of 1946 they made the final payment on their loan, 37 years ahead of schedule!

"I was never able to get a down payment together to buy a farm," Mr. Alexander explained. "If it hadn't been for this program I'd never have owned one. With a loan like this 12 years ago I'd now have one of the best farms in Buncombe County--I had the chance to buy it, but couldn't."

It is amazing to see what they have accomplished in so short a time. They have restored impoverished soil to a productive state. Healthy crops cover former barren hillsides. Weather weary buildings are restored and rebuilt. A dilapidated dwelling is renovated and converted into a cheerful and comfortable home. They have good friends all through the country-side and work toward the betterment of their community.

But to them it is very simple. With restrained pride, Mr. and Mrs. Alexander explain it saying,-"After all, the most enjoyment you get out of life is in fixin things up."

******

A New Water Facility In The Hood River Valley

In a recent report from the state of Oregon is the story of a small but vital Water Facilities Project at Dee, in Hood River County. The Aldridge Ditch Company, Incorporated, (a group of local farmers) have developed 12 farms out of what was once forest, using a small loan made by the Farmers Home Administration.

For years this group of farmers lived on their small farms gradually clearing their land. Their livelihood for the most part was derived from their labors in an adjacent saw mill and the tiny patches of cultivated ground around their homes. Finally they had everything they needed but water.

They dug a mile long ditch on the sloping sides of the mountain through which the waters of Tony Creek could be diverted to their farms. But with all their unceasing efforts, the continual wash from the mountainside filled the ditch with earth deadwood and other debris. After spending their time and over $7,000 of their own money they almost gave up. But one of their number had heard that the FHA could assist in enterprises such as theirs and persuaded them to apply for a Water Facility Loan.

The Farmers Home engineers recommended that a pipeline laid along the site of the old ditch would be a better way to get water to their farms. The water would be more satisfactory for farmstead purposes and it could be applied to the orchards and pastures under gravity pressure through a system of sprinklers. This would permit them to control carefully the amount of water applied to crops and would eliminate erosion.

Farmers generally in the Dee Irrigation District have produced a good quality of fruit and have maintained an excellent standard of living for some 30 years. In this district the farms average some 10 acres or less, but their productivity had been great--the average net profits per acre is from $400 to $500. These borrowers hope their new farms will be equally productive. Money crops their first few years, however, (until the fruit orchards come into bearing) will consist of berries and small truck. Ultimately their group plan calls for 57 acres in pears 17 acres in berries, 8 in vegetables and the rest in pasture. Livestock will probably be a minor enterprise, furnishing only meat, milk and eggs for home consumption.

A conversion dam is now in building that will impound sufficient water further up Tony Creek so that at all times there will be water fed to the farms when and where it is needed.

******

Sound Planning

From a recent memorandum directed to "All County Supervisors in South Dakota" by State Director Arneson, we pass on to you:

> "Too often Supervisors are inclined to apply this planning primarily to the operations on the farm, with very little attention being given to the Home part of the plan. As a result we find that income is inadequate to do the things planned on the farm because unplanned purchases and expenses within the home have consumed substantial amounts. It is not necessarily an adverse condition, solely from the standpoint of the family planning. We probably have not had a full understanding with the family and agreement as to the things to be planned for. When the homemaker sees all income planned for use out on the farm and for debt repayment she knows the plan is not workable. We only fool ourselves. Necessary household furniture, equipment, and supplies will be purchased regardless of the plan. In many instances the disregard for the plan leads to the purchase of items not absolutely necessary.
>
> "Our control of these situations is through a thorough discussion of the family needs, which include both home and farm needs. Get the family's interest aroused in planning for all needs. We then have a way open to us for discussion of the use of income and the priority of items to be purchased. Get the agreement of the family to the complete plan."

******

STATE NEWSLETTERS

ARIZONA-NEW MEXICO

FO borrower Lonnie Cox of Bosque Farms, New Mexico, hit the jackpot again this year, as has become his usual custom, at the New Mexico State Fair by garnering the prize for the Champion Guernsey cow and several others. Another FO borrower of Bosque Farms who won several ribbons at the State Fair for his showing of registered Holsteins was Leo Bauler. Leo also has developed his herd since moving to the project.

******

A group of business men from Greenwood, Sabastian County, accompanied by the county supervisor, Mr. Judd M. Hudson and Mr. W. D. Looper, County Farmers Home Committeeman, made a tour of several farms in the county, and observed the numerous farm and home practices carried out by the families using the services of the Farmers Home. Among those making the tour were C. O. Bell, Chairman of the Sabastian County Fair Association and manager for several thousand acres of Sabastian County Coal and Mining Company land; Bill Lewis, mine operator and owner of 7,000 acres of farm land which is being reclaimed for tenant operators; O. E. Roberts, County Supervisor of Schools; Earl Pryor, Deputy County Clerk and Earl Dodd, Editor of the Greenwood Democrat.

ARKANSAS

Members of the group stated that the trip was very much worthwhile both from the standpoint of giving encouragement to the farm families and making for a closer relationship between the farm and the town. The group also indicated that more visits of this type should be made, and plans are being made for doing this at least once each three months.

******

Field Representative Howard Lawson has turned author and written "An Average FHA Diversified Farm in Hawaii" circular #256 of the Hawaiian Extension Service. It is a summary of the 1947 record books of FO borrowers in the Territory. Law is joint author with the extension horticulturist.

CALIFORNIA

The booklet shows that farmers who maintained a garden and produced much of their food had a higher net income than those who bought all their food. It recommends a four-point home food production program.

******

Colored slides were used to advantage in an illustrated talk on FHA activities given to about 25 members of "The Young Farmers Group" and their friends at Dixon. The pictures used were among those taken to illustrate FO activities.

******

Iowa's results in presenting our program to County Bankers have been so worthwhile that "Tall Corn News" is asking County Supervisors to keep up the good work. Practically every meeting brought out the fact that many bankers do not fully understand just what the FHA can and cannot do. With the Insured Mortgage FO loan program under way there is all the more reason for explaining it to the bankers,--and they are glad to hear about it. It is urged that those responsible for calling these meetings finish the job.

IOWA

******

Of the many field days held during the past few months one of the outstanding events was in Decatur County. Members of the GI Farm Training classes held a soil conservation demonstration on the farm of a veteran who recently purchased his place with an FO loan. Some 40 veterans, most of them inexperienced in the practical aspects of demonstration work, built terraces, moved fences, prepared and seeded waterways, dynamited stumps and engaged in a tractor rodeo for additional fun and entertainment. Bulldozer built a pond and filled a ditch. The Leon businessmen cooperated by closing their places of business during the afternoon. The GI's received some invaluable training and Hubert is now about two years nearer his goal.

******

MARYLAND

The success of the Harry H. Walters family of Charles County, Maryland adds to the already large number, another story of a farmer whose loan, plus hard work brought him unquestioned security.

When the Walters family bought their farm it was almost entirely in brush and timber, only a small plot around the house--1½ acres--being cleared. Promptly they began to carve out of this discouraging looking area their farm of the future. In 1939 the Walters' received an operating loan--later applied for three others. Yet in 1945 these loans were fully repaid. He now has a farm, carved out of the brush and wooded areas with the help of his four sons, that is among the top tobacco farms in Southern Maryland. He has 9 modern tobacco barns, all of them full of tobacco curing; a modern home, machinery shed, a tobacco stripping house and conditioning house with fluorescent lights for grading. This year Mr. Walters planted some 42 acres to tobacco and a conservative estimate places his crop at upward to 45,000 pounds with an estimated value of more than $20,000. To-day the Walters' are debt free, own their farm and another one adjoining, and their net worth is well above $35,000.

******

MICHIGAN

Congressmen Crawford and Michener were visitors at the Michigan County Committeemen information and training sessions recently. To break the ice and start discussion the Committeemen were divided into groups of 4 or 5. Each group was assigned the job of forming questions about some phase of the FHA program. A panel of "experts" from the State Office answered the questions. The Saginaw session was so outstanding in its discussions of farm problems that Congressman Crawford extended his visit thru the full day.

******

Here's one for Ripley. After Supervisor J. B. Poffenberger ran out of funds in the spring of 1947 - several loans were submitted. When new Supervisor Art Hulton received loan money for the 1947-48 fiscal year, he pulled out the unfilled applications and examined them.

One name had a familiar appearance but he couldn't quite nail it down. Upon driving out to the farm of the applicant, he saw the party in question gradually coming nearer on a Ford tractor and then he just gaped. For there on the tractor was none other than his former P. O. W., buddy, David Dickie! Dickie had been a student of Art's in a prisoner-of-war class on Agricultural Credit and Farm Management, and also a bunk-mate on the boat coming home. It's a small world after all!

******

Quote from a Missouri Farm Bureau resolution: "The Farmers Home Administration doing effective work in helping low-income farmers and veterans who are getting started as farm operators. . . One of the greatest services of the Farmers Home Administration is the personal supervision and guidance of its borrowers into a balanced farming program."

MISSOURI

******

When, early in October, the State Farmers Home Advisory Committee met in Syracuse the activities of the State Office were gone over in detail. The study showed that the 1947-48 collections applied to interest exceeded the administrative costs within the state by $131,023.

NEW YORK

******

"Farmers Home Administration Highlights", the N. C. State Office News Letter, relates the following: W. L. Clements and family, FO borrowers of Rutherford County, walked off with many ribbons and over $100 in prize money at the Rutherford County Fair. The family put on an individual booth entitled "We Live at Home" and it displayed the items produced on the farm for home use. It took first place with a Blue ribbon. Clements entered both of his teams of mules and with one took a Blue ribbon, with the other a Red. One of his mules won first place.

NORTH CAROLINA

His son, Hoyte, entered his sow and litter of pigs, a Jersey and Guernsey calf. Result--pigs won second place; Junior Jersey and Guernsey each won 1st place. Another son, Gelane, won second place with his registered Senior Guernsey. Still another son, Bobby, won the County 4-H prize for sweet potato production!

******

For outstanding conservation practices, the Goodyear Tire and Rubber Company awarded a prize consisting of an all-expense trip to Arizona to Rawley B. Conway, an FO borrower in Belmont County....... Clarence Broshear, an OL borrower won first prize in the Third Annual Butler Terracing contest, sponsored by the Rural Youth Organization for the purpose of stimulating a greater interest in soil conservation.......The Huron County USDA Council held a meeting early in December to organize a farm safety program in the county.

OHIO

******

State Director Sorenson believes in getting full mileage out of official statements of FHA activities. Recently the Ohio Farm Bureau called upon him for a detailed report on FHA services and accomplishments. After preparing and submitting the report as requested he had copies made and distributed to State and County Committeemen and others who had asked to be kept posted on program developments throughout Ohio.

******

"The Okie", the State Office Letter dedicated--"That we may more effectively mesh our programs and efforts with those of our neighbors to the betterment of ourselves and them, and to the satisfaction and use of our Area and National Staffs", introduces its December issue with this statement.

OKLAHOMA

"Harry E. McCartney, Supervisor for Kingfisher County, staged one of his FO tours and 61 farms were visited in four days. The number of farms visited each day ran from 14 to 17 and the number of people participating each day averaged about 56.. ......The object of Harry and his Kingfisher County-wide farm ownership group in staging annual tours is to keep all FO farms free from maintenance needs, to personally exchange worthwhile how-to-do-its, and bind closely together in fellowship the entire group." The list of guests on this tour seems to have included every one, official and otherwise, in the County.

******

Last Fall Supervisors Keenan and Ragain, Spokane office, conducted a tour of the area to demonstrate the services and accomplishments of FHA. Congressman Walter Horan participated in the tour. Other members included representatives from the First National Bank, Great Northern Railroad, Jacklin Seed Co., County Extension Agent. The Mayor presided at a noon luncheon meeting, which was also attended by members of Chamber of Commerce.

OREGON-
WASHINGTON-
ALASKA

A great deal of credit goes to Keenan and Ragain for (1) organizing a tour, (2) getting the proper people to participate, (3) preparing an interesting booklet on major points of the tour and (4) obtaining credit for FHA work with farm families.

******

Field Representative Angle remarks: Recent census figures show approximately 25% of the population in this country are farmers who receive 10% of the National income, raise 33% of the Nation's children . . .All of us have the responsibility for creative thinking and planning for low-income farmers in Pennsylvania. We must continue to strive to establish a sound economic business for farm families to whom it has been denied in the past. Many of these folks are veterans who have experience and a strong determination, but little, if anything to work with.

PENNSYLVANIA

To establish a plan for the near casualties of agriculture, it is necessary for us to adopt certain practices not used by credit institutions. Obviously we could not cure these troubles by merely extending credit and using the same methods that caused them. We had to take a different approach so we set out to remove causes. . . Give borrowers the benefit of our professional experience by:

1. Thoroughly analyze the situation
2. Determine the adjustments and improvements to make
3. Record on 14 and 14A
4. Follow up supervision

******

State Director Carson Mertz is using "spot news" radio releases of about one minute in duration that call attention briefly to some one item of interest concerning the services of the Farmers Home to the farm people in the community. They also announce meetings of the State or County officials of the FHA to be held and in some instances they carry a brief statement of the number and amount of loans made in the community.

******

Gene Hansen, Roosevelt, makes splended use of his office space by having a timely exhibit on display. With the help of his "better-half" and Beulah P. Bracken, his office "boss", he's built up a splendid canning and preserving exhibit as the season progressed during the year.

UTAH

Right now Gene reports a display covering the storage of 5 varities of squash. In addition he has had a seed exhibit and one on grain storage. How better can we show and tell people how-to-do-it?

******

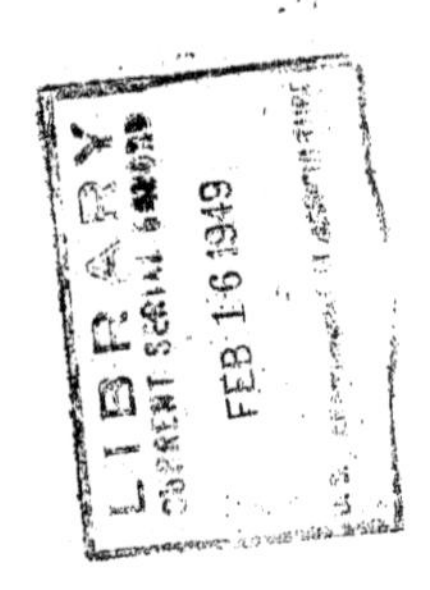

NOTES AND QUOTES

For Administrative Use Only March 1949

USING THE TOOLS AT HAND

Every county office has, or can obtain from the State office, selected pamphlets which explain various programs operated by the Farmers Home Administration. Is your office making the maximum use of these leaflets? Notes and Quotes has compiled a list of ways that County Supervisors or State Directors use these tools. Among the many methods listed below you will find some that can be used to advantage in your county.

A Display Rack For Visitors

In many County offices the leaflets are arranged in a display rack where visitors to the office can see them and help themselves. Persons coming to the office frequently find the answers to many of their questions as they read the leaflet while waiting their turn to talk to you. It saves time because you won't have to answer the questions which the leaflets can answer for you. It makes the interview of greater value to the applicant because he is able to ask more pointed questions, obtain more information on questions which apply specifically to his problems, and apply for only the services which you are able to provide.

Other people who come into your office from time to time also find these leaflets interesting and informative. Many supervisors have reported instances where a newspaper reporter dropping into their office got an idea for a feature story on our program primarily from information he found among the leaflets in the display rack. Other supervisors report that applicants have come to the office because a friend who saw a leaflet in the rack suggested that Farmers Home might have the answers to their problems.

(CONTINUED ON PAGE TWO)

OPERATION HAYLIFT -- IN NEVADA

Success of the Nevada "Haylift" was due in part to alert and hardworking FHA representatives, according to The Pollinator, newsletter for California-Nevada-Hawaii. State Field Representative Eldon Campbell and County Supervisor Mort Domonoske helped get the USDA council of Churchill County to draft recommendations to meet the emergency created by snow and freezing weather. As most of the available hay in the state is produced in a radius of 80 miles from Fallon, it was recommended that a clearing house for hay information be set up in the Fallon Chamber of Commerce Office and a survey be made through the Extension Service and other Chambers of Commerce to determine the supply and need for hay......Supervisor George Campbell was one of the first to fly out of Fallon on an AAF plane to get first hand information on the extent of the storm damage and plan ways and means of helping stricken farmers.

"On his days off, Domonoske volunteered as bombardier on a C-82," the Pollinator says. "The job required great technical skill in bucking two tons of hay out the rear door of a flying box car while traveling at a speed of two miles per minute. Necessary special

(CONTINUED ON PAGE THREE)

INSERTS FOR YOUR LETTERS

Most of the leaflets are shaped to make convenient inserts for your correspondence. Supervisors have found that leaf lets save them time in writing many of their letters. A short, business-like letter referring to a page or a marked section in an enclosed leaflet will often answer the inquiry and add considerable to the correspondents' knowledge of our program. Some county supervisors regularly insert a leaflet whenever they write a "leader letter", because it provides information about work these community leaders should know.

A BASIS FOR NEWS AND RADIO RELEASES

Most supervisors feel that they should supply informatior for the newspapers and radio stations of their area, but a majority of them say they don't know what to write or how to write it. Several have found that by using portior of the leaflet material, or excerpts from the Annual Report, and adding a fev county statistics or a success story of a local borrower they have a release that fills the needs of the local papers.

HANDOUTS DURING TOURS OF BORROW-ER FARMS

One supervisor reports that a recently-conducted tour was very successful because he passed out leaflets before stopping at a borrower's home. The touring Congressmen knew before they reached the farm what kind of loan the borrower had, the conditions under which such a loan was granted, and the results to expect from it. When they saw a live-example of the program about which they had just read, they knew what to look for in order to gauge its effectiveness.

USE THEM AT FAIRS

Many supervisors have found it necessary to prepare, some. times on short notice, a display for their local fair. One effective—and very cheaply and quickly-made—display consisted only of some large home-made posters with figures of progress made by borrowers and some 8x10 enlargements of pictures taken on borrower-farms. In front of the posters was a small table on which the supervisor placed copies of the various leaflets describing our program. Fair-visitors stoppe to look at the pictures, read the story of progress shown on the posters, then took along leaflets to read at their leisure. The supervisor reported that he received several applications which he was able to trace directly to the leaflets at the display. Some of his friends, who he thought knew all about his program, told him afterward that they had learned a lot about what he was trying to do and would be glad to help if he could use them.

HANDOUTS AT TALKS

Every supervisor is occasionally called upon to talk befo some group, usually to tell about the program he is operating in the county. One supervisor who made a good talk before his local Kiwanis Club made it even more effective by passing out a leaflet on each of the major programs he operated—FO, OL, and IM—to each person in attendance. It supplemented his talk, and gave them something they could take along with them to remember and study. Later, when he was contacting the local banker (a member of the Club) to gain cooperation in making an IM loan, he found the banker already "sold" on the program because he had studied the leaflet following the talk.

AS ICE-BREAKERS - FOR INTERVIEWS

One county supervisor has been particularly successful in his personal contacts and he explained his success by saying he "did a little advance spade-work". His spade work was usually to write in advance for an interview at the banker's convenience, saying he would like to "discuss the making of an insured loan to Mr. _______, a farmer who lived at __________." Then he would include one of the IM leaflets so the banker could be prepared to talk about a particular type of loan to a particular applicant. When the banker saw the terms under which the loan was made, and had a chance to study them before the interview, the ice was broken and the supervisor had little trouble concluding the arrangements. The same technique is used by other supervisors who want to explain our program to local veteran leaders, church groups, or prominent agriculturists in their area.

Those are only a few of the many ways supervisors are using leaflets to help them do their job more effectively, more quickly, or more easily. We'd like to have your experience to pass on to others. The method you've found successful may be the very one some other supervisor could use to advantage if he knew about it.

Checklist of Farmers Home Administration publications:

1. Farmers Home Administration, 10 pages, processed March, 1948.
2. Operating Loans, 8 pages, printed July, 1947.
3. Farm Ownership Loans, 8 pages, revised December, 1948.
4. Insured Farm Mortgages, 8 pages, revised July, 1948.
5. Loans for Water in the West, 8 pages, printed February, 1948.

Do you have a supply of these publications in your office? If not, see FHA Instruction 072.1.

******

OPERATION HAYLIFT - IN NEVADA (Continued from page one)

equipment consisted of one very stout rope to keep the bombardier from going out with the bale, and goggles and respirator through which to see and breathe midst the clouds of alfalfa dust whipped back into the plane by the wind stream.........

"In Eastern Nevada the snow was from four to fifteen feet deep on the level during the storms. Following years of heavy selling and reduction of herds during the war and drought conditions on the range last year, this will reduce base stock for breeding purposes to an all time low. In the Fallon area and other valleys of the State, the effects are being felt in a different form. Hay requirements for the winter have been underestimated. Those having to buy additional hay will have to go further into debt at a time when farmers and ranchers should be reducing indebtedness to meet expected lower profit margins........."

The Fallon Standard carried an announcement that "Morton Domonoske, of the local Farmers Home Administration office said in an interview that funds are available in Nevada offices located at Fallon, Reno and Caliente for the purpose of loans to ranchers for the purchase of feed, replacement of livestock and for operating funds. The funds have been made available out of the San Francisco office to aid in the emergency created by storms throughout the State.........."

******

FAMILY FARM URGED BY CHURCH

In announcing "Goals for the Year" the Christian Rural Fellowship Bulletin, (a publication of the Federal Council of the Churches of Christ in America) says that the greatest assets to democracy in this country are the people living in small communities, operating their own farms or businesses and working together for the common social interest. Among the ideals and objectives necessary to insure such a Christian Democracy for rural life are;-

"Family-sized Owner-operated Farms Must be Encouraged.

Soil conservation is related to family-sized, owner-operated farms. We know the farmer-owner-operators are the best conservers of the soil. The trend in the United States has been away from the family-sized farm. A community with a large percentage of owner-operated small businesses and family farms has been shown by recent studies to have more people, more real prosperity, better schools, more and better local organizations, more and better churches, better and more modern homes and less crime and delinquency than one with a large percentage of absentee ownership of the farms and business enterprises of the community.

"Tenancy Should be a Stepping Stone to Farm Ownership.

Young couples cannot gain a foothold on our best lands to-day without some form of backlog such as inheritance or outside financial support. Studies have shown that a young man starting on good land has a better chance of coming out on top than he has on poor land........"

******

AGRICULTURE'S FUTURE LIES WITH LIVESTOCK

The January issue of COUNTRY GENTLEMEN contains an article by Secretary of Agriculture, Charles F. Brannan, who points out the desirability of increasing livestock herds.

"Sometimes we have the good fortune to be in a position where the things we want to do are the things we ought to do," writes the Secretary. "That's the way it is now with agriculture. The major change we ought to make in our agricultural production pattern is to increase livestock numbers and the acreage of soil-conserving grasses and legumes to support them. That would be good for the land, good for consumers and good for farmers.

"In fact, the economic stability of a large part of American agriculture, before another decade ends, may depend upon a big enough increase in livestock numbers to eat what otherwise may be surplus grain, and enough dollars in the pockets of city consumers to buy the resulting increase of **meat** and dairy products. At the same time, increased emphasis on soil conservation will be necessary in order to make sure that production will be adequate in the more distant future."

Administrator Lasseter in his Annual Report for 1948 pointed out several ways that the Farmers Home Administration is helping small farmers adjust to livestock production. "Better organization of farm units for profit and security has been attained on thousands of farms throughout the country.. .....Livestock and poultry have been added, pastures and feed crops developed on farms that were formerly devoted entirely to cotton.....Dairying has been built up as a sound enterprise for the family farm in communities all over the country.........."

******

FARM TOURS

Most supervisors believe that when fields and pastures are at their best is the time to take outsiders to visit a farmer and his family. Then the tourist can observe how the supervision of the FHA is helping solve the many problems of the farmer. But there is a part of such tours that can be done now in winter - and that's the planning part.

Why not plan your tours just as methodically as you help a farmer plan his work?

Go over the list of people that will want to visit borrower farms next summer. Figure out what type of farming they would like to see. Then go over the list of borrowers and pick out the farms and the families that will interest the visitors. Don't pick out only the most successful farmers - your visitors will want to see a cross-section.

Then during the Spring months take the first opportunity to tell farm families that some of the town folks want to come out and visit their place, explain what it is, - pasture improvement, herd management, record book keeping - that they want to see.

You'll find a little careful planning of this sort in advance will guarantee the tours' success.

******

J. GORDON MORGAN

J. Gordon Morgan, former State Director of Wyoming, died on February 9th after a lengthy illness. Mr. Morgan, fifty-six at the time of his death, spent a large part of his life helping rural people. He served as FHA State Director for Wyoming since 1946; FSA State Director for Wyoming from 1941 to 1946; FSA District Supervisor, 1939-1941; and loan officer in Wyoming with the Emergency Crop and Feed Section of Farm Credit from 1935 to 1939.

Mr. Morgan was born in Barnesville, Missouri, September 11, 1893, and graduated from the Macon, Missouri schools. His first position was with Montgomery Ward, in Missouri; but in 1914 he moved to Saratoga, Wyoming. His first Wyoming contact with farming was as an employee of a large ranch near Saratoga. After four years he was made manager of the ranch, and by 1924 had himself become a ranch operator. In 1924 he moved to Rawlins, Wyoming to manage the Morgan Dairy there; but retained his interest in the Saratoga ranch. In 1935 he sold out his ranching and dairy interests to accept employment with the Farm Credit Administration. He served with them as Field Supervisor working out of Omaha.

He is survived by his wife, the former Miss Mary Riddings of Saratoga; and a son.

******

BANKERS SURVEY SHOWS NEED FOR FHA SUPERVISED CREDIT

Some months ago County Supervisors in Michigan queried bankers as to the demand for farm loans from individuals who couldn't qualify for bank loans because of security requirements. They contacted 117 bankers in the State and asked them two questions.

The first was, -"About how many families have come to you during the past year that you think would be eligible for, and benefit by, Farmers Home Administration aid, - and that you turned down?" 102 banks reported 2,427 such families.

The second question was, -"About how many farm families are there in your local bank area who don't have enough resources to get bank loans for operating goods?" About 90 banks reported 6,883 such farm families.

Projecting these figures to include all Michigan banks in rural areas, the State office estimates there were about 7,500 farm families rejected by banks during the past year that would be eligible for FHA aid in Michigan, and about 14,000 other families in the State who don't have enough resources to qualify for bank credit.

******

DISPLACED PEOPLES AVAILABLE AS FARM LABORERS

Some of Europe's displaced peoples who have been admitted to the United States are seeking work as farm laborers. Among the church groups assisting them is the New York State Baptist Convention.

In December, Mrs. Esther McAllester, Home Management Specialist at Ithaca, attended a meeting on this subject, called by Rev. Kenneth Roadarmal, the Convention's Secretary of Rural Work and a former FHA State Committeeman and long-time supporter of our work. It was decided there that various agricultural agencies, including the Extension Service and Farmers Home Administration, would do what they could to help settle these displaced families where their services could be used in agriculture.

While it is impossible for FHA to make them loans, since they will not be United States citizens for sometime, we can notify interested persons of their availability as farm laborers. We understand that they are eager to do such work, are industrious, and many are highly skilled.

Anything County Supervisors can do to help them will be greatly appreciated by interested church organizations, other groups, the families themselves, and by the farmers to whom such families are referred as available sources of labor.

It is probably that some agency in your State has a set-up similar to that in New York to help relocate such families. If not, you can write to Rev. Kenneth Roadarmel, New York State Baptist Convention, 433 S. Salina Street, Syracuse 2, New York, if you hear of any opportunities for them.

****

RADIO

CAN YOUR OFFICE USE RADIO? Just when we begin to wonder if county offices have stopped using radio to report to the public about the work performed by a public agency in comes a flood of letters about FHA radio work.

We get a letter from State Director Space, New York, asking for help with a television show; a call from State Director Newton, Maryland, for help in establishing a new program in western Maryland; a report by State Director Brown, of Minnesota, of a new station which is now broadcasting FHA news regularly; of State Director Beasley, Tennessee, writing in that the powerful WMT of Nashville will use regular FHA broadcasts, and can he get help in working out the program; of State Director Mertz, Pennsylvania and Highfill of Arkansas who supply weekly news items to all radio stations in the state.

Does radio broadcasting have a place in YOUR office? Can you use it to advantage, without too much time and effort on the part of your staff?

Even if there is no radio station which broadcasts from your county, are there ways you can take advantage of radio time to make your job easier by enlisting the aid of others to work with you in solving borrower-problems?

In the past, when radio was confined to those offices where supervisors could go to the radio broadcasting studio or take borrowers to be interviewed, only a few county offices were close enough to make this practical. Today's radio is different, and today almost every county supervisor can find a place where he fits. Instead of bringing the families to the studio, the studio is going out to the farm. And there isn't any reason it couldn't go to FHA borrower farms as well as to those of their neighbors.

Modern radio uses wire or tape recorders which can pick up a message almost anywhere and broadcast it later from the station's studio. The station's radio farm program director will climb into his car, drive out to a farm, talk to the family about their problems, their progress, and their successes, take down the talk on a piece of wire or tape; then carry the message back to his studio for playing at his convenience. The interview can be made at any time, so it can be scheduled when most convenient to the supervisor, the family and the farm program director. If it isn't right, a new interview can be arranged, so bad shows aren't going on the air simply because someone gets tongue-tied or says something without thinking.

Tape or wire recorders aren't perfect--yet. There isn't quite the same fidelity of reproduction that might be obtained from a direct studio pick-up. But actually this is better for farm broadcasts, since it makes the broadcast more realistic, more natural. And you can pick up farm sounds--the squeal of pigs in the barnlot--which might be impossible to reproduce in a studio broadcast.

Wire or tape recorders aren't available in all communities, but it might pay to investigate the possibilities in yours. Most radio stations that have farm program directors have them and use them. It merely means contacting the program director, telling him what you have in mind, and getting his help. Many county agents, today, have some type of recorder, too. So do many vo-ag instructors. And these folk will often be glad to lend you their equipment--or go along and help you use it. By taking them along, you do the double job of letting THEM see your program in action and of getting a recording which others can hear.

There are other ways you can use radio, too, even if you are a long way from the station. Here is how Arkansas does it.

ARKANSAS RADIO NEWS LETTER

In 1948 Arkansas county supervisors asked radio station managers if they could use weekly items concerning activities of the Farmers Home Administration and accomplishments of borrowers. All stations in Arkansas indicated they would like to receive such news.

The State office then began issuing weekly radio news releases to every county office throughout the State. Supervisors give these to their local newspapers as well as local stations. They add local news items regarding accomplishments and activities of the FHA. Thirty-one stations are using this service.

The State Director's Secretary, Mrs. Cash, assumes responsibility for getting the weekly news items prepared. She collects the material from information sent in by county supervisors, from 322 reports, or from State Field Representatives. She usually prepares 8 to 10 short items each week--none of them longer than 100 words.

******

HOME MANAGEMENT NOTES

The December and February issues of "Journal of Home Economics" contain interesting articles by FHA Home Economists. In the December issue Miss Elizabeth A. Rivers, Chairman of the Farmers Home Administration Division of the A.H.E.A., explains how FHA Home Economists decided at a 1948 conference held in Washington that their efforts during 1949 would be concentrated upon four basic family living problems--adequate subsistence, health, money management and housing. The February issue of the "Journal" reprints a paper on "Home Freezers for Farm Families" by Mrs. Esther T. McAllester, Home Management specialist in New York State, prepared for a household equipment course at Cornell University. Mrs. McAllester discusses the many questions involved in whether or not home freezers are justified in the average farm family. She has marshalled the facts pro and con so the farmer and his wife may weigh the costs of purchasing and maintaining a deep freeze unit against the possible saving it may make in the family economy.

******

Miss Gertrude Drinker, Director of Home Management in the Farmers Home, was recently elected one of the Vice-Chairmen of the Home Economics Section of the Southern Agricultural Workers Association.

******

FROM THE STATES

Good Supervision--In Alabama

Since the coming of County Supervisor James E. Lee, to Barbour County, Alabama, the average Farm Ownership borrower's income has jumped by one-third each year as a direct result of a better farming system introduced by Lee.

Barbour is known as a poor-land county - not because all soil types are inferior but because row crop farming, generation after generation, has taken its toll; and erosion and leaching have helped make the land unproductive.

Lee's system involves six basic objectives:

1. Help each family plan their operations according to the type of economy determined to be best for them. Generally this includes reducing cotton and peanut acreage and increasing corn and livestock, including hogs.

2. Select varieties, fertilize, space and cultivate the reduced acreages of row crops according to experiment station recommendations. Half or more of all borrowers are doing this.

3. Build the soil. Use winter cover such as blue lupine, winter peas and oats.

4. Select varieties of corn to provide continuous hogging-off from June to April of the following year.

5. Buy modern machinery and equipment to save labor and for greater efficiency.

6. Balance the livestock program with crops so that present and future labor available on the farm can take care of the operation.

****

Use of Colored Slides Improves Farm Practices—In Arkansas

Generally throughout the country, County Supervisors have made slides to illustrate both good and bad farm practices. At borrowers meetings this means of visual education has been found to be very successful in showing borrowers some of the bad methods commonly encountered in farming and getting them to carry out improved practices.

State Director Highfill of Arkansas, says of the use of slides in his state,—"It has been found that slides made locally by county supervisors serve to generate more interest in improved farming than any other device used in connection with supervision and education of borrowers families." From the numerous colored slides that have been made in Arkansas, a series is being developed for use in all counties throughout the state in teaching pasture development, proper care of livestock and other good farm and home management practices.

****

How One Supervisor Supervises—In Michigan

Michigan State Director Carr recently asked some of his more successful supervisors "how they did the supervision job". Among the answers was the following:

"I have gained the confidence of a few of my toughest cases by actually demonstrating to them that I can help them. On one visit I found a cobalt deficiency in the herd, supplied and mixed a batch of cobalt and fed the first dose. The herd regained their health. Another time the best cow in a borrowers barn was dying from lack of veterinary attention because the veterinary would not come without getting cash on the line. I treated the cow and she recovered. Another family was trying to make the final soil preparation before planting and the tractor was balking. I fixed the carburetor and the tractor went perfectly. Another family was very much concerned over their best apple tree which was dying from pest infestation. I treated the tree and showed them how to apply follow-up treatments and the tree recovered. One 'collection only' case paid up as a result of my spending five minutes to repair their washing machine........"

This and other replies were sent to all county supervisors as part of Michigan's monthly newsletter. State Director Carr said that many of the supervisors who read the letter found ideas in it which helped them.

******

A National First--In Michigan

On February 25, Mr. and Mrs. Clarence Haines, young Negro dairy farmers, received the first insured farm loan made by a Negro lender in the United States. The lender is the Supreme Liberty Life Insurance Company of Chicago and the loan is for the purpose of building a farm house on the Haines' 95-acre dairy farm. Local, State and National leaders honored this young couple at ceremonies that marked the closing of the loan.

Assistant Administrator Stephen C. Hughes who represented the National Office at the ceremonies, pointed out that the Haines family possesses the basic qualities for good farming and good citizenship. He highlighted the three-fold nature of the loan in which the family, the insurance company and the Government had formed a team to increase the family's security and level of living in the community.

W. Ellis Stewart, President of the National Negro Insurance Association and Earl B. Dickerson, general counsel of the Supreme Liberty Life Insurance Company participated also in the loan presentation ceremonies.

The State FHA office at East Lansing headed by Roswell G. Carr, State Director turned out en masse for the occasion. Honors for the happiest person of the day were about equally divided between Clarence Haines and County Supervisor John C. Kenny. The latter was ably assisted by L. J. Washington of the FO Division in Washington and by L. Herbert Henegan of the National office Information Staff.

Clarence Haines was born in Indiana and was reared in Cass County. He is one of 14 children - 12 boys and 2 girls - some of whom have become brick masons, carpenters and electricians. Clarence, last year, with the combined help and talents of his family, built a large and well appointed dairy barn which houses some 20 head of cows. They will use the same skills to help Clarence build the new home.

******

Colored Slides and Public Relations--In Missouri

Missouri State Director Carpenter reports a successful use of color slides to acquaint various groups with the operation of the FHA program. A program was planned for these pictures to be presented to at least one service group in each county. This meant at least 114 showings. In the carrying out of this plan it was found that a minimum of one to fifteen showings were necessary in many of the counties. The results have proved that an illustrated talk with colored slides of actual farming operations on borrower's farms makes a "top notch" presentation.

The Director of Public Relations of the Chillicothe Rotary Club, who attended one of these presentations before members of the club, writes, in commenting on what he called an extremely well prepared program. —"Doing a masterful job of introducing his subject, Mr. Toyne, (from the Missouri State Office) sat down with some beautiful Kcadachrome slides and proceeded to provide the club with one of the best interpretations of the philosophy of your office, as well as its practical application, which I have ever heard. This speaking before a home town group is a tough job—particularly tough when speaking before a group of men who are close friends, who consider themselves more or less experts in agriculture........"

Mr. Leland S. Wood closed his letter by saying that his judgment is not an individual one but is one expressed by several other members including the editor and publisher of the local paper.

******

New Farm Practices—In South Dakota

State Director E. R. Arneson of South Dakota, reports from from July 1 to December 31, twelve hundred instances of doing some specific farm job better than it had been done before, were reported by farm families working with the Farmers Home Administration. These better practices range from better methods of handling poultry to terracing or strip cropping. They are the direct result of close relationships between the county supervisors and families who are utilizing the facilities of FHA. One of the most important functions of the county supervisor is his friendly attitude with all FHA families and the added responsibility of counselling with them in order that each dollar put out in loans for production or for farm ownership shall bring the greatest return possible.

******

Irrigation Project—In Southern Oklahoma

The Daily Ardmoreite tells of the first irrigation project ever to be installed in Carter County in Southern Oklahoma. Previous efforts to grow tender truck crops during the annual mid-summer drouth months have met with little success. Delbert Roundtree of the Farmers Home office discussed the possibility of an irrigation system on the Clyde Minter farm and as a result a water facilities project was started through the cooperation of FHA.

A dam, now completed, will impound sufficient water in rainy periods so that in the season of drouth a sprinkler system will provide water for the tender garden crops. Throughout this section of the State this new trend in farming has caused widespread attention, and, if it produces according to hopes and expectations, it will be the first step for irrigation in Southern Oklahoma.

******

NEWS LETTERS

Arizona

"F.H.A. Briefs", issued from the State Office at Albuquerque, New Mexico, in its December issue, reports on the progress of the David W. Ogden family of Willcox, Arizona, who literally "dug their success story out of a quarter-section of unimproved Sulphur Springs Valley land which they acquired in 1945." It quotes The Arizona Farmer, who told the family's story of success and states that no pioneer family ever faced tougher conditions and no Arizona family ever made swifter progress towards the realization of their dreams. After they had acquired their land they cleared some 50 acres of mesquite by hand. Later they were able to obtain a farm development loan from the Farmers Home. With this loan their going was made much easier and they could work more effectively in clearing the land by less primitive methods than they had formerly struggled with.

******

California-Nevada-Hawaii

The December "Pollinator", carried a brief story from Yuba City, California, telling of two young people, 17 and 15 years old, son and daughter of a Live Oak, P&S borrower, who purchased a subsistence garden for $100 from a retired neighbor. Through produce sales at a roadside stand and the purchases made by three neighboring stores, Walter and his sister received their original investment back in one week. Using their father's truck they then took orders for additional produce and delivered it to customers. In exchange for the use of the truck the children gave their parents fresh vegetables for table use, and tomatoes and beans were provided to fill 100 quart fruit jars. At the close of the season their record book showed a net return to the youngsters of $210.

******

Florida

"Florida News and Views", tells of a different Annual Business and Educational meeting at Lakeland. The meeting was held at the home of borrower Carl Adams, under the shade trees in the Adams' most attractive back yard. Because of the progress made by this family it proved particularly inspirational to the families just coming on the program.

"In five years the Adams family have completely reclaimed an old run down farm, remodeled the house, purchased farm equipment and home equipment to assist them in a satisfactory farm family life." State Director Texada reports, "They are several payments ahead of schedule. The long-time goals they still have to reach are - finish increasing improved pasture, increase improved herd, furnish bathroom and purchase family deep freeze. The entire family is a demonstration in the value of satisfactory farm life."

******

Kansas

State Director Dodge, in his introduction to the December number of "Passing It On", speaks of the 'variables' encountered in making any farm and home plans, and warns that for the year 1949:-"There is danger that some borrowers may believe that good planning and working their plan isn't too important, that good weather and good prices are all that are required for them to succeed Events in the past few years possibly have contributed to these convictions. There are signs that this fair weather planning has run its course and if indulged in in 1949, some families are heading for stormy weather.

"As a prelude to a good job of planning for 1949, a critical analysis must be made of 1948 operations and the record of their results. Such an analysis will point the way to needed changes and adjustments in order to develop the farming system best adapted to the resources of the farm and the family. It will also reveal what farm and home practices need improving and will point out the kind of assistance and the guidance the family will need throughout the year in working their plan. . . . .

"What this all adds up to is a challenge which makes this a good time for each of us to pause and take stock of our talents and reconsider and strengthen our most effective methods of assisting borrower families with the all-important decision-making job of planning their 1949 operations to weather any combinations of 'variables' which may come their way."

******

Louisiana

The Louisiana Grapevine reports that two county supervisors have collected 100 percent of maturities on 1948 loans, both annual and adjustment. Roy Gentry, supervisor in Natchitoches Parish made 1948 loans to 135 families and collected in full from 134 of them. The remaining borrower, who has a $400 tractor loan, is current. In Sabine Parish, Supervisor S. D. Hammons, who also collected 100 percent of all loan maturities, said that the good repayment record was made possible because borrowers used good seed and fertilizer which resulted in more feed than in previous years. Hammons prepared a newspaper article on what his borrowers were able to accomplish with their supervised-credit which was published in the local paper; then mailed each county committeeman a copy of the article and thanked them for their aid in making the collection record and borrowers' success possible.

******

Nevada

In the February issue of "The Pollinator", there is a report from the County office at Reno that in 1938 Charles T. Warr of Yerington, Lyon County, received a loan of $7,000 with which to purchase a 320 acre farm. At that time his net worth was about $4,000. Recently he paid off his entire indebtedness, and Mr. Warr now owns some 480 acres of farm land worth $16,000; $975 worth of food and seed; cattle and hogs valued at over $4,000; farm equipment worth $4,750; household furniture $1,100 and bonds and cash on hand over $10,000, - a total of over $37,000. This year Mr. Warr proposes to build a modern seven-room home - and he has enough money on hand to pay for it.!

******

Texas

"Timely Texas Topics", in its January issue quotes Delta County Supervisor Samuel T. Garrison's County Newsletter as reminding borrowers that there is no business in Delta County that can operate only six or eight months of the year and remain prosperous. Garrison says, "Farming is a business - can farming be profitable on a 6 to 8 months basis? What would it mean to our prosperity if a majority of our farmers had at least one other source of income, - such as laying hens, 4 or 5 good milk cows, some brood sows or 8 or 10 steers to feed out, during this dormant season to help with family and farm expenses."

In these days of higher standards of family living and operating costs, continues "Timely Topics", the one-crop farmer is sure to lose out. Adoption of modern and successful farming practices is essential - and that means diversification and following a live-at-home program.

******

Shortly before the holidays, Chief Justice Marvin Jones of the Court of Claims in Washington was a visitor at the State Office in Dallas. Judge Jones has a long and distinguished record having been a member of Congress from Texas for 24 years. His Congressional service was highlighted by joint authorship of the Bankhead-Jones Farm Tenant Act and as Chairman of the House Agriculture Committee.

******

DID YOU READ

Soil Conservation Service Annual Report

The Chief of the Soil Conservation Service in his annual report for 1948 makes the following observations:

"When farmers decide, in the interests of soil conservation, to shift away from excessive use of intertilled crops to a diversified type of agriculture, many of them must make rather drastic financial adjustments. In making these adjustments—in working out a proper balance between crops and livestock and in acquiring the right amount of properly adapted machinery—credit is essential, or at least desirable.

"The solid results obtained from investments in conservation farming, in terms of increased income, prove that such investments usually pay for themselves and thus provide a basis for the sound extension of credit to finance them. It seems desirable that appropriate steps be taken to broaden the credit structure to permit a more liberal use of credit for sound conservation operations and investments."

Elsewhere in the report, progress of FHA borrowers who used SCS methods were given in case-history form. Many FHA supervisors make their own supervisory job easier and at the same time help their borrowers by bringing the SCS fieldmen into the picture to help with the job.

******

Resolution Adopted at Convention of the National Grange

Congressional Record, Jan. 27, 1949:—(contained in a list of resolutions passed by the National Grange at their 1949 National Convention in Portland, Maine). . . "We pledge our support of adequate appropriations for sound credit for the Farmers Home Administration where such credit is not available elsewhere for assisting capable farm youth and tenants to become owners."

******

Congressman Wright Patman, Texas, in Feb. 14th Congressional Record

"Mr. Speaker, the Farmers Home Administration is making loans to farmers, who want to become farm owners. The applications are carefully screened by local committees for the purpose of making sure that only the deserving and well qualified are granted these loans. The losses to the Government will be practically nil. Through this vehicle, the people, who feed and clothe the United States and a large part of the world, are given the opportunity of borrowing and using the credit of our Government to this very limited extent. They pay interest on the loans and will repay the principal.

"I do not know of a better way to have a happy and prosperous citizenship on the farm than permitting our farmers through their own efforts, including hard work, to own a farm of their own.....I do not know of a better way for Uncle Sam to help deserving people than step up and sign the notes of these farmers, who want to be home owners.

"If the family-size farm is encouraged and preferred to some limited extent over the large farm or plantation operation for profit or speculation, the real people who work will be given a break....."

******

THE PROGRESSIVE FARMER, January, 1949

"The year 1949 will be another profitable one for efficient farmers who are working farms with adequate size and productive capacity. They say you can push ahead with confidence by sticking to a few basic rules that are always sound:

1. Stick to sound farm management practices.
2. Follow a long-time plan best adapted to the farm.
3. Put emphasis on crops and livstock with most price protection.
4. Beware of every high-cost enterprise.
5. Avoid speculation and high-risk operations.
6. Push for high yields per acre.
7. Get big protection per cow, per hen, and per sow.
8. Before spending, figure return and risk.

******

Editorial - THE PROGRESSIVE FARMER, February, 1949

"During the current year, the office of the Farmers Home Administration serving Texas has loaned about a million dollars to tenants for the purchase of farms. During this period, 90 Texas farms have been purchased with FHA funds. The year is only about one-half gone. But FHA is out of loan money. No more loans will be made until another year starts on July 1, unless the new Congress meeting in January makes an emergency appropriation.

"For the year, Congress put up only $15 million for tenant purchase loans throughout the United States. The program is sound. The farms are being paid out far ahead of schedule. It is one of the few social programs on which the Government is getting its money back. There are still thousands of hard working young farmers that need Government help to get farms of their own. It's a good investment for the Government, because it's an investment in better farming and more enjoyable farm life. Once Congress put as much as $50 million a year into the program. It should come back to this amount. An appropriation of $15 million seems just 'piddling around' with a great national problem."

******

SPECIAL AWARDS ISSUE

NOTES AND QUOTES

For Administrative Use Only May, 1949

SUPERIOR SERVICE AWARD WINNERS VISIT NATIONAL OFFICE

Three Farmers Home Administration supervisors were selected to receive Superior Service Awards from the Department of Agriculture during ceremonies held May 16. They were Smith Black, Mexico, Missouri; Hugh Braby, Mason City, Iowa; and Benjamin R. Phipps, Wenatchee, Washington. As part of their "award" the three supervisors and their wives spent three days in Washington as the guests of the National office. Their trip to Washington included, in addition to receiving their award from the Secretary, a conducted tour of the Beltsville Agricultural Experiment Station, visits to special points of interest in the Nation's capital, a chance to see Congress in action, and conferences with Washington FHA officials.

The three day tour, arranged by the Personnel Division and members of the Award Committee began with a meeting in the office of Assistant Administrator Ralph Picard, where the three county supervisors also met Assistant Administrator James E. Halligan and Division Chiefs Stephen C. Hughes and Marcus B. Braswell.

CONTINUED ON PAGE 5

****

AWARD WINNERS

The following sketches of the award winners indicate why the Department selected these outstanding Farmers Home Administration employees for this honor:

Smith Black
Mexico, Mo.

Black was recommended for a superior service award "for outstanding ability and leadership in assisting borrowers to plan and carry out improved farming methods and business practices which have raised their standards of living and secured for them a more stable place in their community."

Mr. Black is considered outstanding in his state for his ability to analyze the needs of

CONTINUED ON PAGE 2

****

THE DEPARTMENT AWARD PROGRAM

The Department award program was established under authority contained in Public Law 600, approved Aug. 2, 1946, to provide a means of honorary recognition for exceptional or meritorious contributions of employees to efficient and constructive public service; and to encourage, through a system of cash awards, the submission of employee suggestions which will result in improvements or economy in the operations or services of the Department of Agriculture.

TYPES OF AWARDS: Three types of honor awards will be bestowed:

a. Distinguished Service Award --Employees whose achievements

CONTINUED ON PAGE 3

farm families, and to encourage borrowers to follow corrective measures. He is unusually effective in teaching borrowers to keep and use adequate farm records. Both the quality of his supervision and the time spent on borrowers' farms are far above the average.

In fourteen years as an FHA supervisor, Mr. Black has made operating loans totaling $900,000 and has a delinquency record of only 6 percent. He has obtained 53 percent more repayments from collection-only borrowers than the average supervisor of his state. He made the first insured mortgage loan in Missouri. None of his FO borrowers are delinquent in their accounts.

His office is frequently used as a training ground for new supervisors, and assistants working under him have proven successful when assigned counties "on their own". He uses his county committeemen effectively in helping him select, review progress of, and otherwise assist borrowers. He has explained the program of the agency to other agencies and groups, and successfully gained their active cooperation and support. He was recently chosen "Man of the Week" by the Mexico Chamber of Commerce. His work with the Audrain County fair has helped establish both the agency and himself as important assets to the community. He was instrumental in organizing the Audrain County Young Farmers Group. Recently the Farm Bureau decided to pay his office rent in recognition of his outstanding work for all farmers in the county.

<u>Hugh Braby</u>
Mason City, Iowa

Recommended for Superior Service Award for "meritorious service to agriculture and rural life by establishing an exemplary record in the execution of his duties." During 10 years as supervisor, Mr. Braby has made farm-plan loans to 870 families, FO loans to 15, reduced his collection-only caseload to 39, and has dropped only 9 borrowers for failure to repay.

In this 10-year period, loans have been used primarily to start families on a sound livestock and pasture program. With loan funds, families have purchased 143 good dairy bulls; 750 beef cows, heifers and calves; 1600 hogs, and 400 ewes or lambs. He has helped borrowers purchase 10 purebred herd sires for dairy enterprises, and 200 purebred heifers, cows or calves. He has encouraged all borrowers to participate in the Dairy Herd Improvement Association, and one borrower has developed to the point where he has frequently been the top-producer in the association. He has helped children of borrowers win top prizes with dairy projects in 4-H work; and was responsible for 80 percent of his borrowers joining artificial insemination associations. He helped develop 3 Soil Conservation Service Districts; and before these districts were established was personally responsible for working out 80 soil conservation plans for borrower families. Mr. Braby has helped borrowers install grass waterways on 323 farms, gully-control measures on 74 farms, drainage systems on 50 farms, contour plowing on 29 farms, pasture improvement work on 235 farms, the use of limestone on 183 farms, and the use of commercial fertilizers on 400 farms. He introduced Reeds Canary Grass on 20 farms, Brome Grass on 76 farms, and improved varieties of alfalfa or clover on 82 farms. He has helped 75 families improve their food storage facilities, and 65 obtain group medical care.

Supervisor Braby is an instructor in a local veteran-training school which includes 135 FHA borrowers as well as many other veterans. He has helped numerous veterans obtain private credit from local banks. He revived the local USDA club and helped maintain its present active status. He also helped organize many community associations.

Benjamin R. Phipps
Wenatchee, Washington

Recommended for Superior Service Award for "meritorious service to agriculture and rural life in the area by fostering and building an unusually complete understanding of the FHA program and objectives among applicants, borrowers, county committeemen and the general public."

Serving continuously since July 1, 1935, Supervisor Phipps is responsible for the operation of the FHA program in an area covering 19.4 percent of the State of Washington, yet leads the state in number of improved farm practices adopted by borrowers, ranks third in home practices adopted. With the fifth-largest caseload in the state, his OL delinquencies are third lowest of all county offices there, and his collections consistently run higher than would be expected from his caseload. He has no water facilities loan delinquencies, an important program in his area.

He keeps borrowers, committeemen and the general public continually informed, through use of tours, newspaper-stories, and radio, of the progress made by families cooperating with FHA. Because he has created a wide understanding of program objectives and accomplishments, he has been able to obtain general approval and assistance in carrying out his program and in covering adequately a widely-spread area.

*****

THE DEPARTMENT AWARD PROGRAM (Continued from page one)

qualify for the Distinguished Service Award will be presented with a gold medal, a certificate, and a gold lapel emblem.

b. Superior Service Award - Employees whose achievements qualify for the Superior Service Award will be presented with a silver medal, a certificate, and a silver lapel emblem.

c. Length-of-Service Award - Ten or more years of service with the Department is deemed to be meritorious service worthy of recognition by award of an appropriate length-of-service emblem. The Length-of-Service Award will consist of a miniature shield and a certificate. The emblem will have an enamel panel of green for 10 years of service, white for 20, red for 30, blue for 40, and gold for 50.

QUALIFICATIONS: Any person shall be eligible for an award for services rendered while employed by the Department. Any employee will be eligible for consideration for the Distinguished Service Award whose achievement constitutes a notably outstanding contribution to agriculture and to the public service. The following illustrative examples will serve as a general guide:

a. Outstanding service to agriculture and rural life
b. Major contribution to science
c. Outstanding skill in public administration
d. Distinguished authorship
e. Notably creative service
f. Heroic action

Any employee will be eligible for consideration for the Superior Service Award as a result of service of unusual value beyond that ordinarily required. The Superior Service Award will be presented for meritorious performance such as illustrated below:

a. Meritorious service to agriculture and rural life
b. Valuable contribution to science
c. Effective public administration
d. Meritorious authorship
e. Unusual courage or competence in an emergency
f. Meritorious service of a creative nature
g. Meritorious execution of duties, establishing an exemplary record
h. Initiation of a suggestion that has resulted in important savings in money, time, materials, personnel, or equipment
i. Initiative in devising work methods that result in important savings in money, time, materials, personnel, or equipment
j. Achievement in improving the morale of employees with consequent improvement in work performance.

Each employee who has completed 10 years of service or more in the Department may be recognized by a Length-of-Service Award after completion of his tenth year and at 10-year intervals thereafter. Service will be computed on a net basis.

<u>AWARD BOARDS</u>: A Board of Distinguished Service Awards is appointed annually by the Secretary. It consists of three distinguished private citizens and three employees of the Department of Agriculture. The Board recommends to the Secretary those persons that should receive Distinguished Service Awards.

A Board of Superior Service Awards is appointed annually by the Secretary. It consists of seven employees of the Department of Agriculture. The Board recommends to the Secretary those persons and units that should receive Superior Service Awards.

The Director of Personnel determines the eligibility of persons recommended for Length-of-Service Awards.

S

NOMINATIONS FOR AWARD: Each agency head will appoint a nominating committee to make recommendations to him. He will submit to the Director of Personnel on February 15 of each year, and at such other times as the Secretary may designate, recommendations for awards to his employees. Nominations for Length-of-Service Awards will be submitted on or before April 1. Any employee may recommend nomination of an employee to the agency head.

PRESENTATION: Presentation of awards will be made with appropriate ceremony on the 15th of May each year (the date when Agriculture was established as an independent bureau in 1862) and at such other times as the Secretary may designate. Distinguished Service Awards will be presented by the Secretary. Superior Service and Length-of-Service Awards will be presented by the Secretary or by the respective heads of agencies of the Department.

OFFICIAL RECORDS: A photostat copy of the certificate awarded to individuals for Distinguished Service or Superior Service shall be placed in the employee's official personnel folder.

*****

SUPERIOR SERVICE AWARD WINNERS VISIT NATIONAL OFFICE
(Continued from page one)

Mr. Picard delivered a personal message to the supervisors from Administrator Lasseter, who was in Salt Lake City addressing a conference of the American Legion.

By 10:00 the supervisors and a number of National office representatives left for the Sylvan Theatre, on the Washington Monument Grounds, where they joined with representatives of other agencies on the stage to receive their awards from the Secretary of Agriculture. All activities of the Department were temporarily suspended so that employees could participate in the program and congratulate the award winners.

Following the presentation and luncheon, the supervisors returned to the Department where members of the personnel staff helped them arrange hotel accomodations, see that return-trip reservations were available, and that the supervisors were familiar with the schedule for the remaining two and a half days. Then most of the group left for a visit to the House and Senate, where they saw Congress in session or visited their Congressmen. In the evening a dinner was arranged followed by an evening tour of Washington by automobile.

Tuesday morning was devoted to a tour of the Department of Agriculture building, then a staff conference in which the supervisors discussed with members of the Administrator's staff their field program and ways Washington could help them in field operations.

Tuesday afternoon the supervisors participated in an FHA ceremony in which they were recognized for their award-winning activities, and then shared the stage with persons in Washington who received length-of-service pins.

Mr. Hughes told why these supervisors were chosen as award winners and Mr. Halligan presented the length-of-service awards. Mr. Braswell completed this part of the meeting by showing a series of slides which illustrated farm and home management methods.

Until closing time, the supervisors visited in various FHA offices, then left to see Washington play Detroit in a big league ball game.

Wednesday was "Beltsville Day" for the visitors. Taken to the Department's huge experimental farms fifteen miles north of Washington the supervisors participated in a conducted tour which took them through the dairy breeding farms, pasture experiment grounds, and swine barns. They heard J. B. Parker and E. E. McDowell tell about recent investigations in breeding dairy cattle; heard J. H. Book tell about predicting milk-producing ability in calves; and learned from L. A. Moore and J. B. Shepherd about pasture improvement and harvested forage work. After lunch at the Log Cabin, J. H. Zeller told of the swine production work at Beltsville, particularly as it applied to the development of the Landrace strain of "lean-meat" hogs.

While the supervisors were at Beltsville, their families were seeing interesting parts of Washington and doing a bit of shopping.

The supervisors "crowded a lot" into the three days; and most of them indicated that they wished it could have been longer; but all were in agreement that the trip was a nice award for their work. All of them agreed that the Beltsville and other experiences had given them new ideas which they would be able to take back to their home counties and use to help farmers live better through farming better.

*****

DID YOU SEE?

The Congressional Record of April 27, 1949, pages 5191-5193, contained information on the Federal Suggestion System that will be of interest to all employees. It is contained in a message to Congress given by Senator Alexander Wiley of Wisconsin. Senator Wiley said, in part:

"Mr. President, everyone talks about Government economy but very few of us ever do anything about achieving it.......

"One of the more immediate ways by which we can achieve economy is by giving every possible encouragement to the suggestion systems already in effect and those that can be put into effect in Government agencies. I have had considerable correspondence with the United States Bureau of the Budget on this theme and I hope to be in close contact with the Bureau further on this subject.

"I have just received a report summarizing the results of the Government suggestion system for the 1948 fiscal year. During that year, 83,000 suggestions were submitted of which 16,000 were adopted. Thirteen thousand awards were made, because these suggestions involved estimated savings to taxpayers of over $15,750,000........

"I congratulate all those folks involved in the limited success of the suggestion system so far. While I have at times, as have my colleagues, made certain criticisms of Government agencies when we felt such criticisms were justified, I feel that it is equally incumbent upon us to give praise where praise is merited. Certainly abundant praise is deserved by all of the employees who have thus far won awards because of their suggestions for Government savings. More power to them and to the agencies in carrying on this vital work in the interest of real economy and efficiency."

In the report referred to by Senator Wiley, the following figures are contained for the Department of Agriculture for the fiscal year ending June 30, 1948:

Number of employees in Department.	67,850
Number of suggestions received	431
Number of suggestions adopted	123
Percent of adoptions	28.0
Number of cash awards made	7
Highest cash award made	$ 50.00
Total of awards made	$ 140.00
Average cash award paid	$ 20.00
Total estimated savings	$1,999.80

The Administrative Analysis Division reports that the program did not get under way in the Department of Agriculture until November 7, 1947; and that this fiscal-year report does not do full justice to the Department--or the FHA--suggestions and cash awards programs. During the 10 months of the present fiscal year, the number of cash awards and amount paid in awards has exceeded by more than 7 times the previous year's totals. Highest award to any agency employee was recently made to Jens L. Ingwerson, of Missouri, who received $100. In the Department, awards have now been made up to $250.

FHA Program During Past Twelve Months:

Number of suggestions received from May 15, 1948 to May 15, 1949	288
Number of suggestions adopted from May 15, 1948 to May 15, 1949	50
Number of Cash Awards from May 15, 1948 to May 15, 1949	43

(a)	$10	29
(b)	20	3
(c)	25	8
(d)	50	1
(e)	65	1
(f)	100	1

Winners Who Received $20 or More:

Bertha I. Yeaton	Laconia, N. H.	County Office	$20
Gladys I. Curtin	Ithaca, N. Y.	State Office	20
Lucy G. Little	Montgomery, Ala.	Area Finance Office	20
Betty Jane Pingrey	Springville, N. Y.	County Office	25
James G. Barrett	Carthage, Tenn.	County Office	25

(More)

Gaylord D. Westcott	Milwaukee, Wis.	County Office	$25
Eric L. Thompson	Red Falls, Minn.	County Office	25
Margaret Jordan	Jackson, Miss.	County Office	25
Frank J. Bartos	LaGrande, Oregon	County Office	25
Sadie R. Daines	Salt Lake City, Utah	State Office	25
Isabelle F. Bartz	Easton, Maryland	County Office	25
George E. Stolebarger	Dallas, Texas	Area Finance Office	50
Wilburn L. Durham	Jackson, Miss.	County Office	65
J. L. Ingwerson	Columbia, Mo.	State Office	100

NOTES AND QUOTES

For Administrator Use Only June, 1949

COMMITTEEMEN HELP SUPERVISORS HELP BORROWERS

No matter how good a job is being done by state or county offices, a better job can be done if committeemen are made full partners in the operation. State Directors and county supervisors have learned that these "part time assistants" can help solve many of their more pressing problems.

ADMINISTRATOR ADDRESSES AMERICAN LEGION ECONOMIC CONFERENCE

Administrator Lasseter and FHA State Directors from the Mid-Western States on May 16 met with policy-making members of the American Legion in Kansas City. This was the fourth of a series of Legion meetings where FHA personnel were asked to tell how Farmers Home is helping veterans.

The conferences were called by the Economic Committee of the Legion and representatives of all agricultural agencies were invited to attend. With the aid of the information gathered at the hearings the Legion will formulate its future agricultural program.

First of the four meetings was held March 21 at New Orleans, La., where Mr. Lasseter and Louisiana State Field Representative Percy A. LeMoine were principal speakers. State Directors from most of the Southern States attended this meeting and in conferences with Legion representatives from their State were able to get better acquainted with the problems of veterans and to show how our program could help solve those problems.

On April 5, State Directors from the Eastern States of Maine south to North Carolina, plus Leo Brown of Minnesota,

(CONTINUED ON PAGE FIVE)

Recently a memo was sent to all State Directors requesting them to report instances where state or county committeemen have gone beyond the line of required duty in order to help borrower families farm better and live better. To date fifteen states have sent in outstanding examples of work being performed by their committees. In the State Newsletters we have found many other examples of similarly helpful work.

The variety of replies suggest that ways which one state or county office find effective might work equally well in others. This month's column, then, is really a collection of reports on what others are doing, prepared in the belief that while some of the practices are ones already used by you, others can be adapted to your area. Typical of the instances reported are:

ARKANSAS Crawford County committeeman Urban Brownlee wrote a letter-to-the-editor piece telling what he had learned about FHA during his first year as a committeeman. In it he summed up his thoughts with the statement "I think the small net cost of this program would be repaid many times over in maintaining and raising the economic level of the families."

*****

Cross County committeeman Robert W. Hall a member of serveral other agricultural

(CONTINUED ON PAGE TWO)

agency committees or farm groups in the county, arranged for an FHA borrower to have his farm done over in one of the recent wave of "face-lifting demonstrations". Mr. Hall told the SCS workers that he wanted to see a demonstration held "on a farm where the farmer actually needs this service badly and where he does not have the financial resources to do it himself."

****

A present and a past Hempstead County committeeman participated in a radio program discussing the activities of FHA borrowers in the county; a committee chairman in Yell County prepared and gave to the press a series of stories about FHA families; a chairman of the Grant County Committee appeared before the quorum court to explain the program of FHA to the JPs, as did committeemen in Hot Springs, Cross and Yell counties.

****

CALIFORNIA-NEVADA Committeeman Henry W. Luhman, of Napa County (Calif.), made a tour of Farm Bureau meetings in the county discussing the work of the Farmers Home. He was accompanied by either the county supervisor or the county agent. Mr. Luhman has also contacted various banks and explained the FHA program so that they now refer eligible borrowers to this agency.

****

Churchill County (Nev.) committeeman Frank T. DeBraga was surprised when he received his first check as a committeeman, and tried to hand it back with the comment "I never charge to help a neighbor". DeBraga's record since becoming a committeeman has really been that of "helping a neighbor". He gets out with his level and helps borrowers determine the best way to level their land for irrigation. He is often found examining borrower's livestock and suggesting ways to make them more productive or to avoid disease. He's even been known to loan a borrower enough to "tide him over" until a crop could reach market or an FHA loan check arrives.

****

Kings County committeeman Edgar B. Stripling attended a tour arranged for FO borrowers and helped the supervisor explain the good farming methods found on the various farms visited. The borrowers saw calves born from artificial insemination; advantages of land leveling; use of well water for irrigation purposes; alfalfa grown for pasture on newly-leveled land; and efficient use of space in the farm home.

****

COLORADO A combined staff-committee meeting was held in March with state staff members, county supervisors, county clerk-typists, state committeemen and many county committeemen present. One purpose of the meeting was to thoroughly acquaint all FHA personnel, including committeemen, of the work of the agency in the state and the emphasis to be placed on improved farming methods. State Director Higbee, in reporting on the meeting said that "a county committeeman, convinced of the scope, need and value of the program is a heavy factor in public opinion. These men left the meeting with: (1)-A new concept of how seriously we take our mission, (2)-that training conferences are not vacations but hard work, (3)-that FHA personnel are kept informed on the economics of the nation, agricultural trends, agricultural research, and use of resources for maximum production, (4)-that FHA is a highly trained fast-moving outfit handling the toughest problem in the agricultural field, namely the 20% or more of the farm families at the bottom of the totem pole."

****

FLORIDA In Holmes County, committeemen Redden Hobbs, Cam Hyman and Fred McIntosh made a tour of all first-year FO borrowers farms to study the practices being incorporated. Eleven veterans and two non-veteran borrowers were included in the tour. The committeemen were much impressed with what they found, and took the opportunity to pass on to each borrower the things they had found useful on other farms visited. Completing the tour, committeeman Hobbs wrote up a piece for the Holmes County Advertiser describing what he had seen. The article mentions such evidences of good farm management as: farrowing pens and weevil-proofed barns on one farm; cotton-poisoning being practiced on a second; and hybrid-corn experimental plots worked out in cooperation with the University Experiment Station on a third.

****

IOWA When the Corydon office became vacant temporarily, the three county committeemen pitched in and took over the supervisory duties until a new supervisor could be appointed. They visited applicants on their farms, worked out plans for farm operations, and in some cases helped the applicants or borrowers obtain better leases for the 1949 crop year.

****

KANSAS When loan repayments proved especially good in Pratt County recently, county committeeman Richard Eads told a reporter about it and a good news story resulted. The story told quite a bit about the agency and its work, about the new insured mortgage program, and about state collections and practices generally. Similarly, in Cherokee county, committeeman Reid told the local press about the new insured mortgage loan program and of some of the loans which had been made to date and another good story appeared. State Committeeman Rev. Gilbert Wolters, professor of sociology at St. Benedict's college, reported to another Kansas paper on a state committee meeting he had attended, stressing that this agency "takes in all the social and cultural aspects of the farmer's life". Chairman Patrick J. Noone, of the Butler-Marion county committee told of the number of applications being received from young farmers and veterans, and told at length why farmers still need the type of credit available from FHA.

****

MARYLAND Caroline County Committeeman Paul S. Ebling was among the group of FO borrowers and committeemen from Talbot and Caroline counties, Maryland who recently toured the Agricultural Research Center at Beltsville. He was particularly impressed with the superior strains of hogs being developed there from crosses of the Danish Landrace with American varieties. The new strains are prolific, averaging about 10 pigs per litter, and about 50 percent of the live weight finishes to the five preferred cuts of ham, loin, bacon, picnic and shoulder-butt.

****

MASSACHUSETTS State Committeeman Carl K. Langenfeld, of Rhode Island, helped make arrangements when Administrator Lasseter was principal speaker at the Rhode Island Agricultural Conference in March. More than 200 state agricultural leaders were present, and heard the Administrator report on the FHA program.

****

NEW YORK After a committee meeting in which the State Director reported how much money had been loaned, how it was used, and the results obtained with the loan funds, Chairman Clarence Johncox issued a report to the newspapers on the use of loan funds and need for additional money if New York's farm families were to be helped effectively. The story, carried in most of New York's larger newspapers, pointed out that "the average total borrower income for the calendar year 1948 was $5,464--an average increase of $1,244" and that "only money for about 33 loans is left, but more than 450 applications are on file now".

****

OHIO Committeeman H. H. Allison, a personal friend and war comrade of Congressman John McSweeney, felt that the Farmers Home Administration could help families more effectively if it did not have to depend upon annual appropriations for its funds. He wrote Congressman McSweeney a friendly letter, stating his beliefs and urging the Congressman to take some action. The Congressman called Administrator Lasseter who explained our program in detail, and helped him gain a better understanding of administrative problems.

****

OKLAHOMA Of Cleveland County committeeman Davis H. Brown, the county supervisor says "He is always on the job of getting things done for his friends and neighbors. A member of the Farm Bureau since its organization, at its meetings he never fails to drive a wedge for the FHA and its work. A member of the Cleveland County PMA for the past eight years, he has always worked to bring the activities of that agency and of FHA into closer harmoney and understanding and has done much to help create the fine fellowship that exists between the two agencies in this county. A member of the Soil Conservation Board since its organization, he has worked diligently and continuously to bring about understanding and a pleasant working coordination between that agency and FHA and whenever merited has interceded for FHA borrowers in getting a maximum of SCS work". The supervisor also pointed out that Committeeman Brown recently was awarded the Skelly Agricultural Award, given by the Skelly Oil Company,--only 10 men in the State have been so honored--for his outstanding work in developing cooperation between agricultural agencies.

****

Committeeman K. Frank Cain has a model farm where he practices all the soil conservation practices approved for the area, and uses it as a demonstration area to show borrowers how to do the job. He is also presently working to develop a source of funds to be utilized by state farmers who purchase farms under our IM program.

****

Payne County Committeeman Odes C. Townsdin, a member of almost every agricultural organization represented in his county and a committeeman for most of the agricultural agencies, has talked on FHA before all these groups; and he is always available to help borrowers through advice or in gaining the cooperation of groups to which he belongs. The county supervisor says "His advice to borrowers has always been good. There are in his county today many small farmers who through FHA services have raised their living standards, increased their incomes or graduated to farm ownership. A considerable part of their success can be attributed to Mr. Townsdin's counsel."

****

The Antlers American carried a lead story prepared by county committeeman Walter J. Adair, which described the work of FHA in developing a dairy program for Pushmataha County. According to Mr. Adair, the agency loaned $56,000 in the county to farmers to help build dairy herds, and as a result 275 high producing cows were brought into the county to become the base for future dairy herds. The agency also helped improve several dairy barns so Grade A milk could be sold. The paper said of Mr. Adair's report that "since its inception the FHA has been largely responsible for most of the dairy farms now in operation. . .and the FHA has supported an agricultural industry that may grow into the biggest thing ever started in the southeast area."

****

OREGON-WASHINGTON Committeeman Keith McCoy, of Klickitat County, (Wash.) took his job with FHA very seriously. Shortly after his appointment he attended a county committee meeting, and listened intently to the procedings. He checked up on the work being done in the county, and was impressed with what he saw. A short time later he learned that loan funds were exhausted, and McCoy knew a lot of young veterans who had applied for credit and now would be unable to obtain the needed funds. He promptly wrote a letter to various veteran groups, explaining the situation and urging them to do something to help these veterans. And he arranged for the county supervisor to appear before various veteran organizations and tell the story of FHA's work in the county. In one of his letters he said "It is distinctly not a gift to the veteran but does provide a channel through which qualified and competent veterans can secure needed funds for their farms. It does not seem unreasonable, therefore, to ask for more substantial appropriations for this agency."

****

SOUTH CAROLINA State Director Kolb, in discussing the activities of various state and county committeemen pointed out that Allendale County Committeman J. Dave Gray, owner-operator of a general store and cotton gin, "uses the contacts he makes with farmers at his store or gin to preach how FHA helps families attain better living and a good repayment record through better farming. He points out examples of progress made by families in the community who received their opportunity through FHA."

****

Mr. Kolb also complimented State Committeemen C.B. Abel, D. W. Watkins, and Frank E. DuBose for their part in making possible the two--white and Negro--paid-up borrower recognition meetings held in the state this year.

****

ADMINISTRATOR ADDRESSES AMERICAN LEGION (Con't from page 1)

Earl Mayhew of Kentucky and Andy Sorensen of Ohio attended the Indiana Legion Economic Conference in Washington to discuss ways our program could be made more helpful to veterans.

The Salt Lake City conference on May 16 was attended by Mr. Lasseter, Q. Kelley, National Field Representative Beals, and most of the northwest State Directors.

In all four of the meetings, Mr. Lasseter stressed the need for good farm management if the veteran is to succeed, and discussed how our supervised credit program could provide this credit-plus-training.

"The biggest road block to the veteran in agriculture is getting the money to pay for his farm, its operating costs and upkeep. The veteran needs money to buy the tools of his trade, to stock his farm, whether he is owner or tenant. He needs money to climb out of the farm-laborer class and become either a tenant or owner. Yet, even with such aids as are now available, the veteran's credit needs are not being met. Because the Farmers Home can make loans only when the veteran is unable to obtain funds from other sources, our program serves as a barometer to determine the veteran's credit needs. Because applications for FHA credit have increased 50 percent in recent months, we know that many of the credit sources are no longer available to veterans. The demand is steadily increasing but funds are exhausted........

"When the American Legion endorsed supervised credit they, perhaps more than any other influence, brought about a recognition of a new type of Government service to its people - that of giving an opportunity to people to become substantial citizens and not to join the ranks of idle or unemployed to tax the social structure of the country.........

"I'd like to throw in just one last thought," said Mr. Lasseter in concluding, "which may, on the surface, seem out of order. While you are working for the betterment of the farm-minded veteran, I hope you will remember that there are many other American families, especially American youths, who need similar solutions to their problems. You are really helping the veteran most when you build the most stable farm economy. While we believe we have a program that will be of help to the veteran, who wants to own or operate a farm and is unable to get the credit he needs, we believe that this same program will help all young farmers. Because the future of farming depends upon the young farmers of today, we want to do our best to start them off on the right road. And your organization is wise enough and powerful enough to see that the bigger job is done."

MASTER VETERAN FARMER CONTEST

The American Legion, Department of Georgia, is sponsoring a Master Veteran Farmer Contest for all Georgia farm veterans having an honorable discharge from World War I or II. Veterans living on Georgia farms and carrying on a farming program are eligible to compete for the cash prizes regardless of whether they are member of the Legion.

****

U. S. SAVINGS BONDS BACKLOG FOR FARM BUSINESS

The Treasury Department is launching a nation-wide campaign to encourage the purchase of Savings Bonds by farmers as a "reserve" to carry them safely through emergency periods. The following release, supplied by Treasury, will give background information which you may be able to use in letters to borrowers, or to discuss with them during farm visits:

"Every farmer needs to save something for a financial backlog for his business. A good farm-management plan takes into account the possibility of occasional cro failure, decline in the price of products, or other emergency. And the thrifty farmer does what he can to save something to tide him over.

"The Farmer needs to put his savings away in a safe place and where they will work for him — earning interest. The safest place is in U.S. Savings Bonds. They are profitable, too. E Bonds held to maturity pay the equivalent of 2.9 per cent compound interest, or $4 for every $3 invested. After 60 days from issue date they can be cashed at the bank, whenever the owner wants his money, for the amount invested plus earned interest. The amounts are stated on the bond. That makes them a handy reserve fund for farm and home security, and for emergency and opportunity."

****

MICHIGAN PARTICIPATES IN CAREER DAY CONFERENCE

A College and Careers Day Conference was held at Hart, Michigan on March 29, and Michigan's administrative officer Frank W. Openlander represented FHA and USDA to explain the opportunities for careers in agriculture.

The entire day was given over to students from participating high schools who "interviewed" the various representatives of agriculture, labor and the professions. In this way the students learned at first hand the advantages and disadvantages of various occupations. The questions brought out what courses of study to follow in high school and college in order to best fit into some chosen field of work. Many of the students were G.I's taking training under the Servicemen's Readjustment Act.

Mr. Openlander was closely questioned on opportunities for and advantages in government services generally as well as supplying specific information on positions in the Department of Agriculture. In his report on the day's activities he said that he believed a number of these students were interested in agricultural careers and that such conferences could result in providing "the right start" for future employees.

W. Lionel Tate, Agricultural instructor at the Hart Veterans Institute, later wrote to State Director Carr thanking him for permitting Mr. Openlander to attend and added "He did a very nice job and we, in the very near future, would appreciate having Mr. Openlander as our guest at one of the G.I. classes in agriculture at Hart Veterans Institute."

State Director Carr said of the meeting ". . .this type of contact contributes not only to good public relations but also to a constructive, long-time program of recruitment for Federal Service."

****

FRESH START FOR VALLEY FARMS

The Arizona Farmer dusts off a musty record of a past to show the progress made since a 5,000-acre tract of land, "Casa Grande Valley Farms", located near Coolidg became a project of the old Farm Security Administration in 1936. The land, once privately owned came under Government ownership as a Co-operative Association. Recently it was divided into 21 farms of between 60 and 160 acres reserved for sale to veterans or any of the original Association members who might want to buy Of the latter group only 4 took advantage of the offer. The remaining 17 farms were all bought by veterans. The Farmers Home Administration sifted the applicants for qualifications and made the loans required.

A few months ago the first of the new owners took possession of their farms and the place began to look like a farm community again. The families have been busy getting in crops and preparing the land. These veterans are interested in different developments,-to grow alfalfa at minimum cost,-and to raise a superior grade of dairy cows.

HOME MANAGEMENT NOTES

NATIONAL

A Nutrition Institute sponsored by the Nutrition Planning Committee was recently held in Washington in Jefferson Auditorium. A morning session was devoted to nutrition education with Miss Eleanore Davis, Nutritionist for the Extension Service and Miss Gertrude Drinker, Home Economist for FHA, discussing the subject: "Rural Education Methods in Nutrition."

Miss Drinker, following Miss Davis on the program, opened her remarks with the statement "Miss Davis told you of the work the Extension Division is doing with organized groups. I want to remind you that from one third to a half of our total population does not belong to an organized group of any kind. Of this total number, a large percentage are farm families, most of whom are in the unorganized group for such reasons as inadequate homes, inadequate clothing, and inadequate transportation. We, in the Farmers Home Administration over a period of years worked with many farm families falling within this group, and I have been asked to tell you some of the ways we have taught nutrition to them.

"To begin with, we have been very reluctant to use the word 'nutrition' with a large percentage of our borrowers, because to many of them the word is a stumbling block. A person's background and educational opportunities must always be kept in mind when trying to help him learn.

"The families with whom we work lack many facilities which make for easier house work, so we capitalize on this. . .Having to cut wood and haul water are among the problems which farm families must plan for. We have taken advantage of this when teaching pressure cooker canning by saying 'If you use the pressure cooker, it will take less water and fuel'. . .

"Diets of many farm families have been limited and lack variety. To alleviate this, we have worked on helping families plan which vegetables to plant. . .we have the responsibility for teaching them how to plant, and how to cook the vegetables. . .

"We have also helped families get year-round gardens. . .another outstanding problem is the supply of milk. The average person likes milk if it is kept cold, but families with low incomes do not have adequate facilities for storage. We have been able to lend money with which to purchase refrigerators or even the old-fashioned icebox. We have helped families improve their economic condition so they could purchase the cow and feed necessary to keep her milking the year round. This is teaching nutrition through the purchase of necessary equipment and supplies. . .

"Most of the teaching we in Farmers Home have done has been on the individual basis, and with our limited personnel this part of our service is being sadly neglected at present. . .But when we talk in terms which the particular family can understand, it's a thrilling experience to show them how and then watch them grow."

****

The American Home Economics Association has recently published a guidance aid "Opportunities in Home Economics", prepared and distributed as a result of the recommendations of the 1944 North Atlantic Regional Conference of the Home Economics Education Service of the Office of Education. It tells how an increasing number of employment opportunities have developed for which home economics education is needed.

The bulletin is intended primarily for school administrators and guidance personnel. It contains information concerning home economics as now taught in secondary schools and the vocational opportunities open to persons with home economics training. One entire page is devoted to the Home Management Division of the Farmers Home Administration and the opportunities offered for a very limited number of home economists with practical rural experience.

****

TEXAS

Mrs. Beulah Smith, State Home Management Specialist of the Farmers Home Administration for Texas reports that the Committee on Food Preservation of the Texas State Nutrition Council, of which she is a member, has prepared recently and distributed two releases on "Recommendations of Home Canning for 1949."

****

VIRGINIA

At a recent meeting of the Virginia Home Economics Association held in Roanoke, Mrs. Ocie J. O'Brien, State HM Specialist for FHA and Vice President of the Va. Association, told the 350 members present of plans of action for 1949-50 for the FHA Department with the Association. Mrs. O'Brien reported that a study on "Progress of Some F.H.A. Families in Indiana and Michigan in Housing and Equipment", made by Miss Mary Settle, former Home Economist with the F.H.A. will be used as a basis for deciding if there is interest among the colleges in Virginia for a similar study in that state. Miss Settle is presently employed as Housing Specialist with the Virginia Extension Division and will be consulted further concerning the application of her study to Virginia problems.

Mrs. O'Brien also brought out in her report plans for interpreting the work of the home economist in FHA to the general public and to other home economists in particular.

RADIO

Weekly radio programs are being conducted by two State Home Management Specialists, Mrs. Carmella Murphy of West Virginia and Miss Ann Eva Russell of Tennessee. Both HMS's have been broadcasting to homemakers more than a year, prepare their scripts on their own time, do a 15-minute show every Saturday, and frequently use FHA material and participants to good advantage.

Mrs. Murphy started out on "The Farmers Program" of WPDX at Clarksburg and received such good response for her information on gardening, canning, nutrition and health, that she was invited to give the same broadcasts on WEPM at Martinsburg, W. Va. and WOHS at Charleston, W. Va. She now does these regularly by transcription, and continues the live show at Clarksburg.

Miss Russell conducts the "You and Your Home" hour on WSM, 50,000-watt station at Nashville, Tenn. She usually has a three-part program comprising current household topics, interviewing a guest, and household hints.

Miss Russell and Mrs. Murphy often pass on to their listeners the practices they recommend to borrowers - and use examples of successful homemaking methods followed by borrowers' wives, in each case crediting FHA.

When the County Supervisor at Martinsburg, W. Va. was holding an FO borrowers event in April, Mrs. Murphy was able to get two advance broadcasts, five spot announcements, and two live broadcasts the day of the event - because she was already well and favorably known to the station.

While their broadcasts are entirely separate from their FHA work, both Miss Russell and Mrs. Murphy make many new friends for the agency and give the public a better understanding of the program through their resulting contacts. Because they are considered "radio authorities" on home and family problems, these increased contacts with civic and community leaders, groups and organizations, often lead to opportunities for better acquainting such people with the FHA program.

****

HOW FIRST TELEVISION SHOW WAS DONE

FHA's first television show was recently put on by Miss Lois Latture, Home Management Specialist, and Glenn Boyd, Field Representative - both of the Arkansas State Office - on station WMCT at Memphis, Tenn. Miss Latture and Mr. Boyd interviewed Mr. and Mrs. Hubert Grant, FHA "Farm Family of the Year" winners in St. Francis County, in what may be the first of a monthly series of FHA TV shows on WMCT.

Walter Durham, Radio Farm Program Director and also agricultural editor of the Press-Scimitar and Commercial Appeal at Memphis, was in charge of the 15-minute weekly farm telecast. For the benefit of other FHA people who may be called upon to do a television program, here's how the show was handled: Mr. Durham started off by naming his four FHA guests and then showing eight photographs of the Grant farm with oral description of each. The pictures were about 8" by 10", half-matte finish, all horizontal in view, mounted on an easel for easy changing, and no more than 30 seconds was spent in comment on any scene.

Then Mr. Durham presented Miss Latture and Mr. Boyd who asked the Grants questions that brought out the latter's major farm enterprises, good farm practices, progress since they were sharecroppers, human interest facts, and accomplishments with FHA aid.

To do a good job of interviewing, and to make a varied lively discussion instead of a stiff, formal question-and-answer period, all four participants thoroughly familiarized themselves in advance with the story to be told. A sequence of the several main points was decided on beforehand, and followed. Miss Latture and Mr. Boyd had a previous arrangement by which each usually, but not always, followed the other with a question directed at either Mr. Grant or Mrs. Grant - with appropriate balance between the two.

Those who saw the show agreed that the farm couple added considerably more than if only one or two FHA officials had been presented. As in radio, most TV stations prefer to have borrowers to "top brass" in the star positions.

****

F114
1/p2

NOTES AND QUOTES

For Administrative Use Only October, 1949

AGENCY COOPERATION BUILDS STRONGER PROGRAM

"There is a very strong liaison between County FHA supervisors and County agents. Without the help of agents of the Extension Service in the counties, FHA could not begin to do its job so well", Administrator Lasseter told a recent seminar of the Extension Staff in Washington

---

HOME MANAGEMENT SPECIALISTS ARE ACTIVE.

During the last fiscal year, an increased activity in the Home Management program was evident in many States, despite the limited number of HM's available to do the job. Part of this increased activity is a direct result of using the HM's to train County Supervisor's in home planning rather than using them to directly contact borrowers. At a recent convention of American Home Economics Association held in San Francisco a committee headed by Home Management Supervisor Mrs. Carmella M. Murphy of West Virginia as Chairman, made a report which told some of the outstanding efforts of Farmers Home Administration personnel in Home Management. A few excerpts from this report show:

Miss Elizabeth Rivers, State Home Economist in Minnesota, has written a statement concerning the work FHA does in the field of nutrition for a publication of the State Nutrition Committee. Miss Rivers also wrote a statement for the Journal of Home Economics on the work of Farmers Home Administration home management specialists.

In West Virginia during the past year 15 broadcasts have been given over various radio outlets in which the family-living phase of the program was reported in numerous news articles in the press

(CONTINUED, PAGE 3)

The same idea is being advanced at many state and national meetings of other agencies in the Department of Agriculture. With State Agricultural agencies and all of the many county and private organizations that exist to help the farmer in better methods for better farming and better living, FHA field workers are finding they can gain cooperation and make their own job easier or more effective.

Such co-operation and better working relations between the Farmers Home Administration and other agencies is welcome evidence that we are operating a program worth supporting. From the State level down through the counties this evidence is steadily accumulating and can be traced directly to the excellent public relations being established by county and state personnel of the FHA. A review of some of these cooperating agreements may suggest ways that your state and county office can be of even greater assistance to your borrowers.

The State Director in Maryland says that "in every county in our area the Extension Service Demonstration Agents work directly with our borrower families." In Minnesota the State FO staff attended a round table discussion with State Extension Service staff members to coordinate mutual methods, problems and policies.

In Virginia SCS and FHA have taken progressive steps towards a more effective

(CONTINUED, NEXT PAGE)

working relationship. Now the county conservationist and the FHA supervisor coordinate their skills and actions to provide a program for the borrower. Here, also, the Chairman of the State PMA committee has instructed his county committeemen to coordinate their activities with the FHA county supervisor so all FHA borrowers may participate in the Agricultural Conservation Program. State Field Representatives and County Supervisors are intensifying their efforts to have FHA families participate in both the PMA and SCS programs.

In Florida, at a joint conference between Farmers Home officials and officials of Institutional On-The-Farm Training Programs, it was agreed that FHA supervisors and Veterans' teachers would jointly discuss, agree upon and prepare a farm and home plan for the coming year in all cases where the veteran-trainee is also a borrower. They learned that more coordinated efforts could be reached on plans for operation of the farm, adjustments and improvements to be carried out by the borrower, the use of funds and the use of income, and believe they now will be able to better the services furnished to veterans, for whose benefit the conference was arranged.

In Alabama relations with all agencies are constantly improving. At present training meetings are being held by Farmers Home on farm planning and at each meeting the local SCS, FS, Ext. Service, PMA men and other experts meet with the FHA state office personnel and visit a farm, make out a complete plan, discuss this plan with the group of FHA supervisors. FHA and its borrowers get the advice of the specialists,--the specialists learn of our problems and how they can help us.

Cooperation is also being developed between FHA and non-government interest. Throughout the country banks are giving thought and taking interest in our insured mortgage loan program, and this leads to a new type of cooperation. The First National Bank of Atlanta, Georgia, for example, is backing FHA in our insured Mortgage Loan program and it is expected we may make loans during the coming year in every county in Georgia. They believe the "supervision" is valuable, and refer cases to us needing it.

Veterans organizations, Civic and service clubs, Fraternal groups have all cooperated with FHA again and again in many ways to develop community betterment. They have learned FHA is particularly interested in veterans, in building better communities or in helping to solve rural social problems. That our work has helped members of these groups, and they cooperate so the same benefits can be obtained by other veterans was related by J. B. Slack, of North Carolina, who said:

"On July 13 I attended a meeting of all Veterans in Warren County who are participating in the Veterans Training Program in agriculture. This meeting was arranged by our County Supervisor, Mr. Ivey W. Day, in cooperation with the instructors for the various Veteran Training Classes and was for the purpose of outlining to Veterans the services available to them through the Farmers Home Administration Program. The meeting was well attended by the Veteran Trainees and the instructors and they exhibited a very keen interest in the services available to them through our program of supervised credit."

Farm organizations in general have been most cordial in their relations and have supported our activities. This good relationship is developing because supervisors or State Directors have spoken at their meetings and explained to them the scope and extent of our program in assisting the very farmers who are often members of their group. For example, State Director Worcester of Maine, was principal speaker of the Washington County annual Farm Bureau meeting in Lubeck, where a large part of Eastern Maine's farmers were gathered at an annual field day. One result of such talks is that resolutions of endorsement are often passed supporting our work.

Cooperation with the agriculture colleges is always helpful, and most states take good advantage of this opportunity to share the job of helping our borrowers. In Georgia, State Director R. L. Vansant, reports:

"Our annual FHA Achievement Day program held at the College of Agriculture on July 14 in connection with the Leadership Institute, and the annual meeting of all personnel in Savannah July 20-22 are meetings that we are proud of. Leaders in health, education, politics, etc., from Georgia and other southern states, in attendance at the Leadership Institute, were surprised and gratified to observe the progress that FHA borrowers are making in better farming and better living, as they listened to the program at this meeting. We in FHA were also gratified to mix and mingle with more than 150 farm families who have actually gotten results in carrying out our policy of better farming and better living. This meeting, and other observations that we have made, convinces us that many of our borrowers in every county in the State are actually doing better farming and better living. You have observed from the newspaper clippings and other items that we have sent to you, that the press found something to write about at this meeting. In other words, these farmers told the story of success, and the press was glad to get it.

Our Achievement Day programs in the future will be based upon progress that borrowers make a better farming and better living. We are now working on the criteria that will be used in determining this progress. Three meetings will be held in the future, one for North Georgia at the State College of Agriculture, one for South Georgia at the Abraham Baldwin Agricultural College and Coastal Plains Experiment Station, and the third one at the Ft. Valley College for Negroes. These institutions are working with us 100 percent."

From the evidence at hand the Farmers Home Administration realizes that there are many agencies that appreciate the human values in our program. That they cooperate so extensively is a gratifying recognition that a good program is worth supporting.

******

HOME MANAGEMENT SPECIALISTS ARE ACTIVE (Continued from page 1)

showing how the home economist has helped many families who are making good. Talks have been given to FHA State Committeemen interpreting the work of the home economist in West Virginia. At a recent meeting of the West Virginia Home Economics Association Mrs. Murphy interviewed eleven home economists over the radio in order to arouse interest in such a career.

******

In Oklahoma, Home Management Specialists frequently appear before civic groups to interpret their work to others. Such presentations were made to Lions Club,

Kiwanis, Chamber of Commerce, Veterans Groups and Garden Clubs. Personal contacts have been also established with the home economics departments of various colleges in the state.

******

Miss Lois Latture, Home Management Supervisor in Arkansas, represents the Farmers Home Administration by serving on the following State Committees:

State Consumer Speaks Project
State Nutrition Committee
District Home Economics Committee
Plant-to-Prosper Executive Committee
Secretary, State Home Economics Association
State Judging Committee for the Plant-to-Prosper
and Balanced Farming Contest.

******

The Home Management Specialists in Tennessee are making a series of slides that will tell the story of the four phases of family-living now being emphasized. These slides will be used in public relations work when home management supervisors appear before other agencies, home economics meetings, Veteran Auxiliary groups, County Committee training meetings and FO meetings.

******

At the Rural Atlantic Exposition held October 4-9 the Virginia State Home Economics Association had a booth, "Careers for Home Economists". Mrs. Ocie Jones O'Brien, State Home Economist was in charge. She used as a backdrop the picture from the state career bulletin which she had blown up to 2 x 3 feet and a list of the different fields of work for home economists, which included Farmers Home Administration. Home Economists were in the booth each day to talk to interested persons and register them so they could follow-up with visits to these girls by local economists.

******

Mrs. Ester T. McAllester, home management specialist, took part in a panel discussion at the College of Home Economics, Cornell University, the purpose of which was to inform girls in the Home Economics Department of opportunities within the U. S. Department of Agriculture. She also participated in a panel at a local high school to present vocational opportunities in home economics.

****

Miss Virginia C. Coker, Alabama home management specialist, reports that home supervisors have explained the FHA program to State Home Demonstration Agent for Extension Service, presented the FHA State Plan of Work to the State Home Economics Association at the annual fall meeting last October (1948), and has contacted the various local agencies to explain our program and enlist their services in order that county supervisors might call on them for assistance. The FHA program has also been explained to several district meetings of Veterans Administration.

******

Miss Marion V. Hester, Kansas state home economist, reports that special effort was made to assist county supervisors in making contacts with other agencies to determine how their services could be made available to borrower families. This naturally gave her an opportunity to interpret the job of the home economist to others. She also states that she gave talks to various agencies and groups concerning the work of the home economists in the Farmers Home Administration. Miss Hester is a member of the Kansas Home Economics Association council and was elected vice president of the Kansas Home Economics Association for this year.

VETERANS HELP FO BORROWER BUILD CONCRETE DAM

Francis Krattenmaker, farmer of Swift County, Minnesota, needed credit to purchase his farm. The making of the loan, however, depended upon an extensive program of repairs requiring certain concrete construction. He couldn't borrow enough to buy the farm and also carry out the construction.

The veterans' classes were preparing to give a demonstration of some of the newer methods in concrete construction and how to make cement. To give the boys a practical lesson, the supervisor arranged for Krattenmaker's farm to be used as a demonstration. Over 100 veterans went to work, built concrete footings, a curb, manger, feed alley and platform for cattle in the barn. On the granary they built a shallow reinforced beam; in the poultry house they utilized concrete blocks to repair and raise an old foundation and they added a water-seal floor.

The Krattenmaker farm was a beehive of activity as the boys operated the cement mixer with the skill of old hands. Within two days they had completed one of the finest cement jobs in the area. Mr. Krattenmaker, through this valuable cooperation of all hands, secured the necessary construction work to obtain an FO loan, ---and the 'boys' learned under practical instruction how to do a good cement job.

WATER FACILITY LOAN REVIVES ARIZONA'S OLDEST IRRIGATION SYSTEM

The Cottonwood Ditch Irrigation System, one of the oldest in Arizona and in usé since the early '80's has been completely reconditioned through a $42,000 water facilities loan obtained from the Farmers Home. The Cottonwood ditch extends from the Verde River to Bridgewater, a distance of 6½ miles and furnishes water for 750 acres divided into 50 farms.

Concrete flumes have entirely replaced the old, rotten wooden ones that entailed costly repairs each year; inverted siphons have been installed; manholes have been provided to facilitate the pumping of water for fire purposes in the town and a 400-foot open ditch has given way to buried concrete pipe. With this project complete the farmers of the fertile Verde River Valley will be able to increase their crop production and make a much more efficient use of irrigation.

RADIO

When Mrs. Ocie Jones O'Brien, Virginia Home Management Specialist, needed a radio script for use with a borrower's wife on a small-town station, she prepared it in such a way that it would be easily adapted and used with other borrowers' wives on other stations throughout the State.

She and the State's other two Home Economists expect to do a series of live broadcasts on the basis of this script, as they travel around over the State helping County Supervisors, and find suitable "interviewees" among FHA farm women.

FROM STATE DIRECTOR'S REPORTS

KENTUCKY

In Kentucky each county has a Rural Church Council, and State Director Mayhew has asked county supervisors to contact Council members informing them about FHA aims, methods, and accomplishments - and opportunities for FHA-church cooperation.

LOUISIANA

F. L. Spencer, Louisiana State Director, has asked each Supervisor in the State to put on his "must" list the preparation of a brief resume of the program activities in his parish, and give it in a talk sometime before his Police Jury meeting. Spencer says that "Inasmuch as the jury is the governing body of each parish and made up of public-minded citizens, we feel this is a very important matter. We think it is of such importance that we are requesting the Field Representatives to assist you in presenting your material to the police jury."

MISSISSIPPI

A County Supervisor and a County Agent, (idea inspired by the Supervisor) gave a joint broadcast over WNAG at Grenada, discussing the separate responsibilities each has for helping farm families in the area. The broadcast was intended to clarify the jobs each performs, and explain how those jobs supplement rather than overlap each other.

****

In Covington County, on the farms of FO borrowers, Glenn McDaniel and Neel Mooney, two different series of slides are in course of being developed. Slides made on the McDaniel farm will show the production and harvesting of 2 acres of Dixie #18 Hybrid corn and will be made at three different stages of growth and at harvest time to show yield. To be shown at FHA meetings, accompanied by carefully prepared data, these slides will bring to the observer actual color photographs showing conditions at date of planting, fertilization, land preparation before planting, cultivation, and harvesting. The steps in establishing two acres of White Dutch Clover and Dallas grass pasture will be the subject of the slides being developed on Neel Mooney's farm.

OHIO

A tour of three Farm Ownership and one Operating Loan farm was conducted by FHA in Southern Ohio, with the State Extension staff and resident professors of the Ohio State University College of Agriculture participating. County agents in surrounding counties within the area were invited to attend the dinner meeting, followed by a discussion on farm planning on the places visited.

OREGON

During a recent field trip to Oregon, Miss Gertrude Drinker, home economist for the National Office, was guest of honor at a dinner attended by leading home economists in Portland. Included in the group were home economists from the Dairy Council, Oregon State Department of Welfare, Multnomah County Department of Welfare, cafeteria manager for the Pacific Telephone and Telegraph Company, Legion Post #1, Child Care Committee Chairman, and the incoming President of the Oregon Home Economics Association.

At the conclusion of the meal, Mrs. Amy Larkin, State HM specialist, showed pictures of progress being made by borrowers families in Oregon and concluded the show with the set of training slides developed by the National Office. Since half of the group was made up of farmer home management supervisors, the interest was keen and the desire for "More FHA" was quite evident.

TENNESSEE

State Home Management Specialists, Miss Ann Eva Russell, Miss Mary Hagner, and Miss Rubye Smith are making a series of slides that will tell the story of the four phases of farm family living they are now stressing among borrowers, and that can also be used when they appear before (1) borrower meetings, and other outside organizations, (2) county committee training meetings, (3) home economics groups, (4) veterans auxiliaries.

****

Tennessee, the second State in the nation to hold an FHA television show, featured a disabled veteran with an FO loan for its second TV cast over WMCT with Walter Durham, Farm Program Director, in charge. Tennessee plans a monthly show.

WISCONSIN

State Director Schmidt reports that his staff is working up a set of themes or ideas around which to build photographic sequences with pictures taken by camera-minded Supervisors. The pictures, slides, or movies will illustrate good and poor farm practices - and will have "variable continuity" depending on the purpose for which they are shown. Some series will be used for FHA meetings, some for public gatherings where Supervisors are called upon to speak.

$1000 TO $20,000 IN TEN YEARS

Mr. William C. LaRue, Associate Editor of the Carolina-Virginia PROGRESSIVE FARMER, told in the July edition how the G. C. Mason family of Oconee County South Carolina, got an FHA loan and as a result of supervision increased their worth from $1,000 to $20,000 in ten years.

Quoting Supervisor Walter B. McKinney who worked with the G. C. Mason family, LaRue explained they were just one of the hundreds of families in South Carolina who had utilized the services of the Farmers Home to buy and pay for their farm. Back in 1940, after spending six years as a tenant on the farm, Mr. Mason arranged for a loan from the FHA and in 1947 he repaid it in full, becoming the owner. Up to 1940 Mason had been a cotton grower but he switched to a new plan,--one where soil conservation and supervision played a great part in establishing fertile pasturage, grain crops whereon livestock--which now became his main diversion,--were fattened and readied for market.

"Beef cattle is the main thing", said Mr. Mason, "I just sold 50 head a few days ago. I also sell dressed calves at 50 cents a pound to people around here for their freezer lockers. I got $1,000 for surplus hay and barley last year and I sell some chickens, eggs and truck. I try to sell something just about every day except Sundays."

IT HAPPENED IN MISSISSIPPI

You have probably read the July 30, edition of Collier's in which Quentin Reynolds, famed War Correspondent, lecturer and traveler has written about the Farmers Home Administration, its farm-ownership program and what the end result is for the borrower. Having read of an annual pay-off meeting of Negro borrowers, the interest of Mr. Reynolds was aroused and he was sent by Collier's to find out for them just how the one-crop farm in the deep South is giving way to diversified farming. Reynolds wanted to see for himself if it was possible under the program of the FHA, for a Negro family, having obtained a character loan from the agency, to make good and in a comparatively short time become farm owners, --not tenants or sharecroppers as they had been for generations.

Objectively Mr. Reynolds approached his task, and in the development of his story, the reader can note how he becomes more and more interested in his subject, --the result being commendation for Farmers Home Administration.

THE SOUTH'S FORGOTTEN MAN

Hodding Carter traces the life of 'Clint Bickham', a typical FHA borrower, in the Saturday Evening Post for August 20. He says "While owners laugh at or mistrust the Farmers Home Administration, they cannot dispel the reality of the diversified, supervised acres, the painted little homes, the electric lights and refrigerators, the cows and chicken yards and hogpens, the truck gardens and the laden shelves in the kitchen."

******

In its Bankers Farm Bulletin, the Federal Reserve Bank of Atlanta paid special tribute to the Farmers Bank of Monroe for its service to agriculture in Georgia. The leaders behind the work of the Farmers Bank are C. R. Bradford, President of the bank and George Baker, Manager of the Farm Service Department. Mr. Baker, trained in agriculture and banking, attempts to analyze and understand the problems of the farmers in his area and help them to work out effective financial aid plans.

"Indicative of its wide interest in better living conditions, the bank loaned this year $20,000 for home and farm beautification," the Bulletin reports; "Five years ago there were only six dairymen in the county; to-day there are 52 dairy farms and the Farmers Bank is financing 40 of them." The Robert Strickland Memorial Award, awarded annually, previously was received by the Farmers Bank as the Georgia bank showing superiority in the field of farm credit.

******

EDITORIAL

The Home-town paper really believes in the program which Georgia supervisor Harry Neal, of Morgan County, is operating. In an editorial in the Morgan County News for October 1, 1949 appeared the following:

IT'S AN OPPORTUNITY

"Harry Neal's farm program is doing a whale of a good job. You can go anywhere in Morgan County you want to and you will find some fellow that his farm purchase program has helped to get a start towards buying a farm. Making home-owners and landowners is the best way to make good citizens.

"There would be no worry about this country going communist if most of our citizens owned their homes and farms. It is extremely hard for a young person to get a start and many of them would give up in despair because of the long hard years of strict economy and hard work that it takes but if they had a chance and a little help they could go.

"We believe that this farm financing program is a wonderful opportunity for our young farmers to get a start. We know of many young men that have bought themselves a farm and a home through Mr. Neal's agency and most of them are well on their way to owning their farms."

******

A VET PUBLICATION TELLS OUR STORY

From National Amvet, Washington, D. C......"When Wilbur Carpenter of Madison, Missouri, made the final payment on his farm purchase loan last fall, two other things happened of great significance to all veterans interested in farming.

"He became the first veteran to repay in full exclusively from farm income a government farm purchase loan; and by repaying the forty-year loan in three years he proved conclusively that the veteran--if given practical on-the-farm training and necessary credit--could make good as a farmer."

VICE-COMMANDER VISITS VETERAN'S FARMS IN COUNTY

Courier-Index, Mariana, Ark......"On Wednesday, June 22, Leonard W. Moody, National Vice Commander of the National American Legion, accompanied Woodrow Cearley, Lee County FHA Supervisor, on a routine supervisory trip to veteran farmers who purchased their farms with a loan through the Farmers Home Administration. Six veteran FHA landowners were visited, including the first and last loan made to veterans by the FHA. On each of these field visits, a review of the Farm and Home Plan was made with Mr. Moody and later, while walking over the farm, improved farming practices listed on the Farm and Home Plan were observed in operation......

"Mr. Moody stated that he was amazed at the vast amount of technical assistance rendered the veterans by the FHA and other cooperating agricultural agencies. He asked each of the veterans if they were satisfied with their farm and the help they were receiving and in every case he received an affirmative reply with such comments as 'Had it not been for the FHA Program, I would not be here as an owner today. It was my only chance for a set-up like this.'.

"Mr. Moody remarked on the trip by saying, 'I have seen today the best example of veterans becoming well established in business of their own since the end of World War II.'"

SUGGESTION AWARD WINNERS HONORED IN LOCAL PAPERS

When Gladys Highfill, Oklahoma FHA employee, received a $100 check for her suggestion for bettering office procedure in processing loan applications, she became the second FHA employee in the Nation to be handed a three-figure award. The Daily Oklahoman carried her picture admiring the Certificate she received at the same time from State Director Ozbirn, with a nice cut-line explaining why she was so honored.

Miss Highfill was not the only recent FHA employee to see her picture in the local papers as a result of her award-winning suggestion, however. Mrs. Betty D. Grubb, clerk-steno in Richmond, Virginia, smiled happily for the Richmond Times-Dispatch photographer as State Director Delano handed her the check. The story which accompanied her picture says her suggestion saved Uncle Sam $500 annually.

JOHNNY HAYHURST WHO LEFT HIS EYES IN MANILA SUCCEEDING AS AN AREA FARMER

By Dan Ryan

Kalamazoo (Michigan Gazette, May 29)......Four years ago Pfc. Johnny Hayhurst was one of the first handful of American soldiers to enter Manila. The day after entering the Jap-infested city Pfc. Hayhurst was hit in the face by a ricocheting rifle slug. That slug destroyed his sight completely but failed to dent his greatest possession, courage!

For nearly two years Johnny Hayhurst lay in Army hospitals from New Guinea to Connecticut. During those years he began the long job of learning how to live all over again. About two years ago Johnny returned to his home town, St. Joseph, Michigan. He married the girl he had known before the war; he purchased the farm he wanted--a 209-acre spread near Glendale--and he became a farmer.

Faced with the problem of stocking the farm with milk cows to assure a steady income, Johnny went to the Farmers Home Administration. "Frankly, I didn't know what to say at first," said J. B. Warner, County Supervisor for the FHA. "Johnny had had no farm experience, he'd been a machinist before the war. Even if he hadn't been blind it would have seemed a bad risk to lend him money. But he was so sincere and confident that we took the chance. In six months he has almost earned the price of his stock. It's amazing".

HOW AN ILLINOIS BANK SERVES FARM CUSTOMERS

The Farmers and Merchants National Bank of Nashville, Illinois urges farm customers to keep careful accounts, according to an article in "Banking" for September. To further this help to farm clients, the Bank furnishes to each customer a special record book by which the farmer can easily estimate his financial condition.

Last December the bank added a monthly "local" letter prepared by the work unit technician of the Soil Conservation Service and the bank also advertises in a monthly newspaper issued by the local Farm Bureau in a column written in a friendly, confidential manner about items of a local nature.

More than 500 farmers in the Nashville area receive a regular farm letter from the bank giving them the low-down from the National vantage point.

STATE NEWS LETTERS

AREA FINANCE OFFICE II.

In the June issue of "The Teller", State Director, Mr. Julian Brown of Alabama calls attention to the little recognized fact that "Finance" is one of the most important single divisions in Farmers Home and is responsible in a large degree for the subsequent success of all FHA farm families.

Not alone, says Mr. Brown, does Finance apply it's energies to the space problems of County Offices; to the providing of proper forms, nor to the keeping of records of advances and re-payments. "Without adequate county office space," observed Mr. Brown, "providing a satisfactory place to work, the employees who are dealing with borrowers cannot perform their jobs satisfactorily and cannot, in a manner desired by all employees, properly represent the Administration in the eyes of the Public.

"County Supervisors help farm families in many ways; they process the initial applications for loans; they bring the County Committee to the farm to evaluate the situation and to report on the ability of the applicant to make good; they acquaint the State Office of the transaction. But in the final analysis the Finance Division processes the many loan documents; they keep up-to-the-minute records of funds advanced and the repayments against such advances. They process innumerable forms and their work affects the well-being of thousands of farm families."

KENTUCKY

The first copy of Kentucky's state News Letter, "Frontlines, Headlines in Agriculture", has a brief sketch by State Director Earl Mayhew telling how during some fifteen years Farmers Home or its predecessor agencies have helped farmers on family-type farms to do a successful job of farming. He outlines Kentucky's program and plan of work for 1950 and his firm belief that FHA personnel will be of greater service to a larger number of farmers.

A leading article explains the survey of FHA borrower-progress currently being made by the State Director which survey clearly shows that farmers cooperating with FHA on a planned and supervised basis do improve their farming and gain much benefit from such improved farming. In another report, "Better Farming in the FHA Program", Mr. Mayhew emphasizes the importance of getting farm ownership and adjustment loan borrowers to improve their systems of farming and to carry out approved farm and home practices; he states further that in loan making and supervisory activities, quality of work will be placed ahead of quantity.

MISSOURI

Recently, "The Gregg Writer", a magazine for secretaries, stenographers and typists, carried a story about Miss Florence C. Murphy, employed by the Farmers Home Administration in Missouri. Lois Lamme tells of the unusual career of Miss Murphy in Civil Service and comments;- "The offices welcome Miss Murphy's visits not only because she is an office-style Florence Nightingale, but also because she is so very pleasant. She has been able to help and criticize the persons she trains, so her personality ranks with her shorthand and typing skill and with her knowledge of government office procedure as a valuable tool for success. The story of Florence Murphy is, therefore, a story of successful service......"

The State News Letter from Missouri further states, -"We already know we had a wonderful, talented girl in Florence, and we take considerable pride in knowing that her work has been recognized outside of the FHA and rates publication with her picture in the magazine mentioned." "Notes and Quotes" is happy to report this excellent recognition to one of our personnel and we hope to learn that we have other "office-style Florence Nightingales" in our midst.

MASSACHUSETTS

The American Legion, Department of Massachusetts, has an Agricultural Committee, purpose of which is to assist veterans to better farming. It is planned to have a Legionnaire in each Post designated as agricultural adviser to whom veterans can go for help and advice. Since FHA plays such an important part in assisting veterans to buy farms and operate them, each of us should know some Legion members so that they will know to whom to send veterans. Legionnaires, many of whom are successful farmers, can be of assistance in aiding veterans in their farming. Let's not overlook this good bet and let's get acquainted!

MISSISSIPPI

"Magnolia State News" in its issue for June, tells the story of Ensign Jesse Leroy Brown, age 23, Hattiesburg, son of John and Julia Brown, borrowers from the Farmers Home, who is the first Negro to receive a Commission as a U. S. Navy Aviator. His civilian education was obtained the hard way, he supported himself through Ohio State University by working as a waiter and boxcar loader for the Pennsylvania Railroad. Then in 1948, after thorough training in Naval Aviation Schools, with advanced flying and electronics, he was assigned to the Navy's Fighter Squadron 32, and was commissioned aboard the Carrier Leyte while at sea.

The Browns operate a farm near Hattiesburg and during the past four years they have made considerable progress in acquiring livestock and farm equipment. They have taken great pride in sending their children to school and are especially proud of Jesse Leroy's accomplishments.

NEW HAMPSHIRE

Carrying on a one-man veterans program, Stanley E. Hunt, County committee man for Belknap County, has been instrumental in bringing in six veterans to the Laconia office and of these two have received loans to date. Mr. Hunt performs yeoman service in assisting Supervisor Bernard Davis in his relations with the Soil Conservation Service.

NORTH CAROLINA

One of the most valuable connections a County Supervisor may maintain in serving his community is in knowing the local newspaper editors and in keeping the papers informed about what the Farmers Home is doing in the public interest.

A practical method is being used by Supervisor Walter J. Smith, of Franklin County, North Carolina who finds that in taking along a reporter with him when making calls on borrowers, a good story in the local paper is usually the result. As a further help to the reporter he encourages his county office clerk to prepare a few stories of local interest that may be used by themselves or as a fill-in for the reporter's use.

SOUTH CAROLINA

"Palmetto Pickin's", in it's August issue, tells of valuable information that may be picked up on farm tours, and says, that the eye is a better teacher and more willing than the ear.

"There are always numerous examples of good practices on the farms in your county,--or better yet within the immediate community,--which both FO and OL borrowers would find interesting and beneficial." Some suggestions vital to a tour:--

1. Advanced planning so that individuals will assemble promptly at the designated place.

2. Advanced planning for a bus or truck into which all passengers can be loaded with the leader so that all will see and hear the what, when and how of the different demonstrations visited.

3. The lunch or dinner period, while a Dutch affair, should be handled in the same manner; that is, reservations should be made in advance and the group never permitted to wander at will until adjournment.

The son of an FO borrower, Billy Witherspoon, age 13 and a member of the Future Farmers of America judging team of the Elim High School in Florence County, was declared the highest individual scorer at the Dairy Field Day on May 21.

******

James Archie, Chester FO borrower, is State winner in the Negro Soil Conservation Contest for 1949. James will compete for Southeastern honors at the Log Cabin Soil Conservation Jamboree in Georgia.

******

Chesterfield and other counties have adopted a method of boosting farmers and keeping the public informed as to Farmers Home Activities. This weekly column, "Traveling Around with FHA," is used by a number of local papers and is prepared by each County Supervisor citing interesting items of community news.

For instance, in Chesterfield County, -"Mozell Coward of Ruby Route 2, proves the wisdom of not depending on one cash crop," - "Mr. Fenderburk also practices

diversified farming as he grows melons, tobacco and cotton as cash crops......"
"William Little of Cheraw Route 1, who purchased his farm in 1943 and paid the loan in full in three years by hard work and good farming practices grows and sells truck......as his cash crops."

WISCONSIN

"Doings in the dairy state" of Wisconsin under the program of the Farmers Home is discussed in the first edition of the State Newsletter, "The Badger Cream Line," for August 1949.

The format of this first issue shows good continuity in its 'build up', as it brings into immediate notice observations from Staff members pertinent to important phases of our program such as 'better farming for better living' and the insured mortgage loans.

One section quotes excerpts from letters received from borrowers telling of their progress and appreciation of what FHA has been instrumental in doing for them. County Committeemen are given a brief word commending them for their assistance in the operation of the FHA program.

Lightning Source UK Ltd.
Milton Keynes UK
UKHW012016021218
333216UK00014B/2451/P